WE
ARE THE
CHAMPIONS

# We Are the Champions

Inspiring Stories of Children Across India
Who are Champions of Change

RASHMI BANSAL
DEVENDRA TAK

BUSHFIRE PUBLISHERS

First published by Bushfire Publishers LLP 2020
(Venture by Rashmi Bansal) Core House, Off CG Road,
Near Parimal Garden Ahmedabad 380006



ISBN: 978-81931821-3-0
10 9 8 7 6 5 4 3 2 1



Typesetting by: B2K Bytes 2 Knowledge
Bushfire Logo design by Surbhi Jain
Official photographer: Raghav Chowla
Additional pics by authors
Section separator images from © Shutterstock
and www.vecteezy.com
Book design by Haitenlo Semy

Printed at Thomson Press (I) Ltd.

*Dedicated to*

Dushyant Tak
Nivedita Bansal
And all other children. In the hope that
they will read this, and other books.

# CONTENTS

# AUTHORS' NOTES

## Devendra Tak

When you read the true accounts of these 15 children from across 10 states of India, you will discover what a privilege it has been to have met them. Since 2004, when I joined the International Committee of the Red Cross (ICRC), the most beautiful part of my professional life has been to meet a lot of amazing children from around the world in a variety of contexts. As a communication professional with the ICRC and, later, the International Federation of Red Cross & Red Crescent Societies, CIVICUS: World Alliance for Citizen Participation, UNICEF and Save the Children this has undoubtedly been my greatest privilege: to go deep into their stories. To all of these wonderful organisations, I am grateful for providing me the unique opportunity to spend time with hundreds of children, including these 15.

Working in the Development sector (jettisoning a career in journalism when it was still worth it and where I met and worked with Rashmi Bansal at 'The Independent' in the early days of our careers), has led me to this lush landscape, where my vision has become broader than I could have ever dreamt. I have become strongly aware of the gap between me and others who did not have the simple privileges that I took for granted.

Having followed the success of Rashmi as a best-selling author, the thought did arise if I should venture into putting together a book and Rashmi herself did occasionally prod me. Nothing came to my mind for many years that could be useful and interesting, worthy of attempting. But slowly the idea of documenting the stories of children, who were not only coping with extreme challenges but who had the fortitude to think of helping others, began to take shape.

The children featured here are struggling against the highest odds to create positive change for themselves and – more importantly – for others. Given that 40 per cent of India's population is children, and the estimate that by 2020 India will become the world's youngest country with 64 per cent of its population in the working age group, we do need to pay attention to how these children are being brought up today, more than ever before. If India's children are illiterate, unhealthy and unsafe, there will be direct consequences for the nation and the world at large.

The children's stories were awe-inspiring and there was no doubt that it was important to share these as widely as possible. It took a little effort to convince Rashmi to partner for this initiative but everything ultimately worked out -- and here we are!

**New Delhi**
**January 2020**

## Rashmi Bansal

I started working at 'The Independent' when I was in my third year of college, just for a lark. Most of the journalists ignored me and treated me like a kid (white hair carried a lot more weight back then!). But Dev (as all his friends know him) was different. He went out of the way to include me in conversations, give me encouragement, as well as tips on how to navigate office politics.

For making a teenager feel that she had it in her to be a good journalist, I owe Dev a debt of gratitude. And that is my primary motivation for collaborating on this book.

My knowledge of the work Save the Children does was quite scanty before I took up this project. But as I got deeper into the subject, I was amazed and fascinated.

Much of my previous work is centred on entrepreneurship - where there are concrete and visible goals. Even the social enterprises I cover tend to be those whose impact can be quantified. But as I met several of the children featured in this book, I realised that social change is far more complex.

It is easy to create laws but very hard to implement them. Almost every social evil from child marriage to child labour to dowry is illegal. But these practices have not ended. And they never will, unless the cry for change comes from within. This is the beauty of the 'Child Champion' model which empowers boys and girls to become the conscience-keepers of their communities.

The training module 'Lalita and Babu' used by Save the Children has been instrumental to the success of this program. It makes difficult subjects interesting and accessible to kids as young as 11 years of age. I was surprised to learn that this life skills education handbook was originally used in Sweden and then adapted for India. A topic which, I believe, must be included our national school syllabus!

The initial groundwork for this book was done by Dev, I came in later. I thought I would simply 'storify' it, using the audio and video material he had collected. But that didn't feel right. So I went out and personally met as many of these children as possible. In the slums of Mumbai and Delhi, in Jharkhand and West Bengal.

The most memorable of these trips was to Bandudi village in Kandhamal district of Odisha, which is about 6 hours by road from Bhubaneshwar. I was an honoured guest at the home of Jhulima, a young tribal girl fighting against child marriage in this remote area. The dignity and self-respect with which this family leads a frugal life moved me deeply.

It is my hope that this book creates a bridge between rich and the poor, city-bred and village-bred, donor and recipient. The wall of 'Us' and 'Them' will then crumble and fall.

When we rise together - all 1.3 billion of us - we will be a Force the world has never seen.

There is strength, purpose, purity and plurality, in development for all.

**Mumbai**
**January 2020**

LADENGE
We Will Fight

**ANOYARA KHATUN**

Age 23, Sandeshkhali (West Bengal)

# BREAKING DAWN

At the age of 13, Anoyara was trafficked to New Delhi by a greedy uncle. After being rescued she has saved hundreds of children from a similar fate.

Anoyara's village was no stranger to cyclones, which tore apart lives and families.

"But for me, bigger than cyclone, was the death of my father… it changed everything."

Till then, Anoyara Khatun had experienced no hardship in life. Hers was a normal family in rural Bengal, with many siblings plus aunts and uncles nearby. A home of modest means but one which could afford the occassional maachch-bhaat*. Abbu (father) was very affectionate towards all his children, and more so the girls.

However, not being very educated, abbu had married off his two oldest daughters at an early age. It was simply what everyone did, at that time.

"But then abbu realised that child marriage is wrong and he let my other sisters study upto class 7."

6 months after the wedding of his fourth daughter, abbu passed away. Anoyara was just 5 years old at the time.

---

* fish-rice meal which is very dear to Bengalis.

Even as they dealt with the shock and grief, pain of a different kind emerged. The pain of hunger. Now who would feed this large family? Anoyara's brother was not mature enough to shoulder the responsibility. Ammi (mother) was illiterate. Somehow, the family eked out an existence. On many a night Anoyara went to bed hungry.

One day, a distant relative came to her home and spoke to ammi.

"Sister, I know you are facing difficulties… I want to help you."

The man offered to take Anoyara to Kolkata, where she would stay with a good family and do housework. But he gave an assurance that they would treat her well.

"My Anoyara is getting free food and education - why, she is a lucky girl!" thought ammi.

She had faith in chacha's* words, and his promises. So it was that at the age of 11, Anoyara set off from Sandeshkhali village, the only home she had ever known, with hope in her heart. It was the month of April, she remembers, just after completing the class 6 examinations.

---

* uncle, usually father's brother

From the border of Bangladesh, where Sandeshkhali lies, to the city of Kolkata, is a long journey. What Anoyara did not know was that her journey would be much longer.

"Instead of Kolkata, they took me to Delhi. I was locked up in a big house…" she shudders, as the memories come flooding back.

Reliving the experience is very painful. Suffice it to say there was hardly enough food and certainly no education. A lot of verbal abuse. Emotional scars. And even physical violence. One incident she clearly recalls is the owner throwing hot water towards her. Luckily, she moved out of the way and did not get burnt.

There was another girl - a couple of years older - trapped in the same house. Both spoke Bengali but never dared to speak to each other. Such was the terror in their heart.

But the day hot water was thrown at Anoyara, the girl came forward to protect her. She was beaten badly for this.

"I could hear her screams and cries…." says Anoyara, with sadness in her voice.

This ordeal continued for 4-5 months. During this period Anoyara had no contact with her family. Her mother still believed that 'all is well'. One day, however, ammi was surprised by a knock on her door. It was a lady from an NGO who was calling to make some enquiries.

"How many children do you have?" she asked.

Ammi said that she had 4 married daughters and one who was working in Delhi. The lady from the NGO raised her eyebrow. When she learnt that Anoyara was just 11 years old, an alarm bell went off in her head. This was exactly why the Pavnar Dhagagia Social Welfare Society* was conducting a door-to-door survey.

"Please call your daughter and find out how she is, where she is," the NGO worker told ammi. "And let me know what she says."

The woman came the next week and the week after, each time with the same questions, to which ammi had no answer. Now, she too, was feeling worried. More so, when the NGO people revealed that many children from the area were sent to big cities on false promises. They might be exploited as house-help, or even worse.

---

* local partner of Save the Children

"More than 100 girls were trafficked to red-light areas last year… so we are also worried about your daughter."

After much persuasion, ammi shared the contact details of the 'chacha' who took Anoyara with him. Pressure was mounted on this man, to share the little girl's whereabouts. Chacha was involved in a number of other illegal trades and thought it was best to wash his hands off this museebat (headache).

So he did a bit of negotiation and somehow got Anoyara out of the employer's house. And on to a train headed back to Bengal. He left Anoyara some distance from her village, knowing he would not be able to face her mother. But little did he know that even the little girl would curse him loudly.

"Because of you. I have suffered so much… I will expose you!" were her last words to him.

Although Anoyara was happy and relieved to be home, she was also sad, and angry. Sad, because often she thought of the other girl, still trapped in that house. Angry, because often she asked the question - why did this happen to me? This anger was often expressed, in an explosive manner, even to those trying to help her.

"I look forward to an
Earth where every girl
will have a pair of wings ...
so she will be able
to fly freely under
the open sky."
UN

GA

I don't want any other child to have to go through what I have.

"Where were you, when I was taken away and abused?" she would cry, shaking with emotion.

Although Anoyara rejoined school, her heart was not in studies. She felt it was pointless - too much damage had been done.

During this difficult time, the staff at the Multi-Activity Centre (MAC)* were extremely patient and understanding. They involved her in various group activities, gave her tuitions and a whole lot of extra care and attention. Manab Ray, who was heading Save the Children in West Bengal, noticed how fearless and outspoken she was.

"If only her anger could be channelised in a constructive manner," he thought.

It took time and mentoring but gradually, Anoyara's rage subsided. The past could not be undone but what about the future of children, just like herself? At the centre, she met many children who had been rescued, some of whom had faced horrific abuse. They sat with eyes downcast, filled with shame, unable to utter a single word.

---

* joyful learning spaces for school dropouts who need mentoring to rejoin the system

It took a lot of counselling for these kids to open up and share their stories, which were shocking to the core....

A young girl did not know how to use the electric iron. She had burnt her employer's sari by mistake. The lady pressed hot iron on the front and back of her body as a punishment.

"I was working as a maid but whenever saheb had a party he would force me to do dirty things with the guests," revealed another child, who was raped by multiple men.

"My pain is nothing in comparison," thought Anoyara.

There were boys who were forced to work in mines, and sexually exploited. There were girls who had been forced to work in massage parlours and sexually exploited.

Listening to these stories made Anoyara's blood boil. However, she was able to channelise her anger into doing something more constructive. Anoyara became a member of the Children's Group in her village. The main activity of the group was to spread awareness and to do this, they conducted door to door surveys. Children who were not going to school could thus be identified and steps taken to re-admit them.

At the same time, the children also became like 'guardians' of their own areas. They knew who was coming and going, which homes had young children. Any shady characters immediately came to their notice. On a rainy evening in July 2009, 3 strangers were thus spotted entering the home of Jamila*. A 15-year-old girl who had once been trafficked, rescued and brought back to the village. Once again, she was in danger...

"We must go and create a ruckus, prevent this from happening!" decided the children.

A band of boys and girls headed to Jamila's house, alerting other group members along the way. But when they knocked on Anoyara's door, her mother refused to let them in.

"I won't let my daughter out of this house," she declared.

To which Anoyara replied, "Ammi - what if it was me instead of Jamila... and no one came forward to help?"

The message found its mark.... Ammi could only bless Anoyara - and her friends - as they scurried off to complete a noble task! By this time it was pitch dark. The children realised it would be wise to take along a few elders. Now

---

* name changed

Jamila's family had got wind that some people were heading towards their house. They told the visitors to leave quietly, from the back door of the house.

But the chaps had been spotted and were given the chase. They were caught by the scruff of their necks and taken to the local anganwadi centre. Where they were tied up and given a thrashing. Later, the sarpanch got their wounds treated and then asked them to leave.

"If you ever show your face here again, you will not be as lucky!" he warned them.

The incident shook up the whole village. The real and present danger of child trafficking was now understood, along with the modus operandi of such goons. It was also a turning point for Anoyara.

"I felt a new sense of confidence.. that if we are in a group, we can stop such things from happening!"

Impressed by the bold and fearless way Anoyara stood up to her own mother, the children elected her as their group leader. Very soon she was working not only in Sandeshkhali but in the neighbouring villages. Over the next 3 years she mobilised children in these bastis to form groups.

By 2012, there were 80 Children's Groups - with at least 15 members - taking up the cause of children through awareness drives and other activities.

In the villages* covered by these groups, no child now goes missing. More than 250 cases of trafficking have been prevented, along with 40 child marriages. Over 100 child labourers were rescued while 200 dropouts have been brought back to the formal school system. And who has done all this? The children themselves.

"I learnt from Manab Da that change is possible... but it takes time... and a lot of hard work."

Anoyara started forming Children's Groups while still a schoolgirl. She continued to lead this effort while attending college. Along with her studies and social work, Anoyara also had duties at home and gave tuitions to earn some extra income. Her day began as early as 4 am, with little time for rest or recreation... but unlimited energy for the cause!

In fact, a local newspaper bestowed the title 'Don of Sandeshkhali' upon the teenage Anoyara Khatun. And well, it was not all in jest....

---

* 80 villages of Sandeshkhali, Sabdeshkhali and Minakhan blocks in West Bengal.

The model of Children's Groups to prevent trafficking was pioneered by Save the Children and implemented by youth leaders like Anoyara. Such was its impact that the model has been formally adopted by the West Bengal government. Under ICPS (Integrated Child Protection Scheme) every block in every district of West Bengal now has a Child Protection Committee.

"I am happy that more and more children are being saved from a life of suffering!" says Anoyara.

For her outstanding contributions, Anoyara Khatun was first felicitated by the Chief Minister of West Bengal, then the Prime Minister and finally, the President of India*. What's more, she represented India at the United General Assembly (UNGA) two years in a row - 2015 and 2016. It was a moment of great pride and joy, to represent her country at such a prestigious forum.

"I also realised that the problems we face in India are not ours alone..."

---

* Anoyara received the Nari Shakti award from the President of India in 2017

On the very first day of UNGA '16, Nadia Murad* took centrestage. She related the ordeal of being captured by ISIS, held as a sex slave, and her lucky escape. Since then, Nadia has been a tireless spokesperson for Yazidis and girls across the world, who are victims of trafficking and sexual abuse.

"As Nadia spoke, I could see the glimpses of my past as a child...," says Anoyara, choking up.

Both young women are beacons of hope or, as they say in Bangla, 'jolonto pradeep' (burning lamps). Working to dispel the darkness in the heart and ignorance in the mind. That leads to girls still being trafficked and abused, and permanently scarred. In her address to the UN General Assembly, 19-year-old Anoyara made this passionate appeal:

"I look forward to an Earth where every girl will have a pair of wings ... so she will be able to fly freely under the open sky."

A world that is fair, that is just and above all, safe. For children everywhere.

* co-recipient of the 2018 Nobel Peace Prize

*After a long, dark night, there is a new dawn*
*After a long, hard fight, there is a new norm*
*May our children grow up to be brave and free*
*As God and as nature intended them to be*

**ANJU VERMA**

Age 17, Doulatpur (Haryana)

# THE AWAKENING

Why should girls and boys be brought up differently? Anju set the ball rolling by asking her own mother this question

*Why should girls and boys be brought up differently? Anju asked her own mother this question, and then, the rest of society.*

Anju grew up in rural Haryana, where boys are fawned over and treated like little lords.

"*Waise to mere mummy-papa bahut achche hain* (my parents are good people) but my brother was the pampered one."

It was in small things that she felt the difference. Like mummy expected Anju to take permission before going out to play with her friends. And she had to help mummy with housework. But *bhai* could do as he pleased. Mummy's explanation was always the same: "*Ladka sab kuch kar sakta hai, ladkiyan to paraayi hain*'. Boys can do everything, girls are born to be married.

For in the heartland of India, dominated by the Jat community, women still wear ghunghat* and play second fiddle to the men.

Nevertheless, Anju was lucky enough to be born in better times. She was going to school, a privilege her mother never had... And one afternoon, as Anju skipped home after a long day in class, she heard the faint echo of a

* a veil to cover the face

loudspeaker. Oho, there is some program going on in the chowk (village square).

*Bachchon ke bhi adhikaar hotey hain?* (Do children have rights?)

"*Chal,* let us find out what is happening," she said to her friend. "*Mazaa aayega*... (it will be fun)."

In the middle of the chowk was a large van decorated with colourful posters.

"*Sabhi bachchon ke adhikaar hotey hain*.... All children have rights," said a pleasant young voice over the loudspeaker. "Do any of you know what are these rights?"

"*Nahin pata!*" replied the children in the audience. "Tell us, please!"

The voice on the loudspeaker went on to explain: whether small or big, rich or poor - every child has an equal right to study, to play, to lead a healthy and safe life.

*"Aur jab ladke ko yeh opportunity di jaati hai aur ladki ko nahin to usko bhed bhaav kehte hain...* When boys get certain opportunities but girls do not, that is wrong, it is called discrimination."

Anju and her friend glanced at each other – *yeh to hamare saath bhi ho raha hai.* It was the story of their lives too! The program ended and Anju went home. But she could not sleep.

'Why does my brother get to eat before me?'

'Why does he get so many nice clothes to wear?'

'Why are girls not allowed out of the homes to play with each other?'

The video van people were saying one thing, but her parents were just the opposite. *Ab kaun sahi, kaun galat...!* (Who is right, who is wrong?)

After a great deal of reflection, Anju reached the conclusion that her parents were acting wrongly. But *unko batayein kaise?* Talking about such a thing was not easy. So, while Anju helped her mother with the daily chores, she slipped in a story or two about some 'friend' whose parents were violating child rights.

"*Pata hai, unke upar case bhi ho sakta hai!*" (A case can be registered against them.)

In this indirect manner, Anju introduced her mother to a very new idea. But on Dussehra day, she got the courage to really speak her mind. During this festival, an effigy of Ravana is burnt - symbolising the triumph of good over evil. And as they watched the spectacle, Anju made an unusual request.

"*Mummy, main aapse vaada chahti hoon.... ki aaj se mere aur mere bhai ke beech koi bhed bhaav nahin karoge.*" (From today, promise me that you will not discriminate between me and my brother.)

Her mother thought for a moment and then said, "*Theek hai - vaada kiya...*" (All right, I promise.)

Anju could not believe her ears. Was mummy joking, or was this change of heart for real? Well, to her surprise, mummy kept that promise. And Anju's heart swelled with joy.

At the same time, she was sad that other girls were not as lucky. Her classmate Shalu* always came to class without doing her homework, and was punished for it. When asked why she played truant, the girl replied that she had

---

* some names in this story have been changed, due to concerns regarding privacy

no time to study. There were other responsibilities - like making chapatis and looking after the livestock.

"If you are worried about my schoolwork… go talk to my parents. Make them understand!"

Now, at first, Anju was hesitant. Would these grown-ups listen to her? But then she thought - 'If my mummy could change, why not others?'

So she did take the bold step of approaching Shalu's parents. But not only did they rebuff Anju, *aur do baatein suna di* (she was attacked verbally).

"*Tumhare mummy-papa ne to tumhari patang ki dor dheeli chhod rakhi hai.*" (Your parents have given you too much freedom. You will spoil our daughters, as well.)

But Anju did not take their words to heart. She went a second time. And a third time. Because, despite the hostility, at least they were *listening*. On one such visit, Anju took her uncle along.

"*Hum aapko samjhaane aaye hain…* " they said. "But you should also know there could be a case against you - with Rs 50,000 fine and 6 months in jail."

"My parents have given me the opportunity to study, play, go out but when I look around the village - at my friends - I find that they do not have these opportunities."

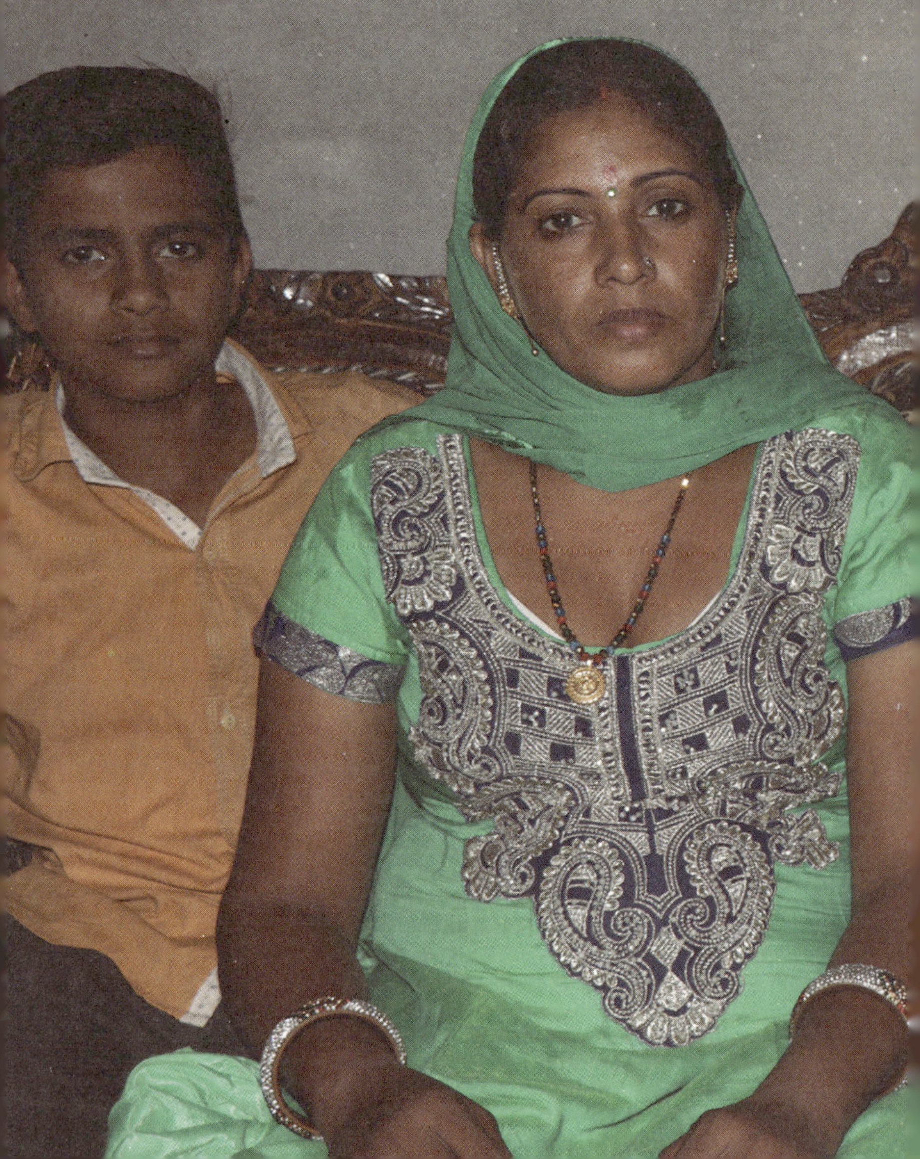

Presented to
Anju Rani
In appreciation for her inspiring talk on
"Bringing Meaningful Change"
at TEDxPune 2017.
Presented by,
Team TEDxPune
TEDx Pune
UNRAVEL

Finally, the parents realised *ki badalna hi padega* (we have no choice but to change). Shalu now came to school with a smile in her step, and all homework duly completed.

This encouraged Anju to approach the mother of Geeta, another classmate with the same problem. Here, what worked was an emotional appeal.

"Aunty - every day the teacher says your daugher is dull and stupid... *aapko acchha lagta hai aapki bachchi ko daanta jaaye*?" (Do you like that she gets scolded like this?)

The solution was simple - give the little girl less work and more time to study. The mother agreed and in a few months, Geeta's marks jumped from 33% to 57%!

"*To uske baad mera bachchon ke liye kaam karne mein interest hone laga.*" (I got interested in working for more and more children.)

Anju became a part of the Bal Samooh (Children's Group) in her village. In fact, she was elected as the leader. Seeing her passion and enthusiasm, Anju was sent for training to Sirsa and got involved with a state-wide campaign against child labour* in 2016. But to stop kids from working in the fields, it was important to speak not only to parents but to the zamindars (land-owners).

"What can we do?" they would say. "The parents bring their children to work."

Anju told them that those parents were doing something illegal. And if under-age labour worked on their farms, the zamindars would be equally guilty in the eyes of the law. And thanks to this awareness campaign, a large number of land-owners took a vow: 'We will not employ any labour under the age of 14 on our farms.'

But victory comes at a price. Many a tongue wagged in the village, undermining Anju's efforts.

"Her parents should keep an eye on her… why is she interfering in our business?"

The harsh words did upset Anju. But she reminded herself of her goal - to work for the welfare of children like herself. *Ab koi mujhe sahi maane ya galat.* (What people think doesn't matter.)

---

* The campaign was called '*Komal haath kalam ke saath*' (Tender hands should hold a pen).

Luckily, her own parents were extremely supportive. Anju has gone to Delhi and Bangalore for training and she even delivered a TEDx talk in Pune. In fact, when she returned, dadi (grandmother) distributed sweets to everyone and Anju was felicitated by the sarpanch and also at the district level.

The confidence she has built through all this work inspired Anju to start her own NGO in October 2017. 'Bulland Udaan' aims to work in all areas connected with child rights. For the first meeting, Anju's target was to gather around 20 volunteers. But more than 60 turned up! However, there was much hard work to be done, mostly in the hot sun...

"Many dropped out... we were left with only 20 team members. *Par hum lagey rahe.*" (We did not give up.)

The volunteers conduct door-to-door surveys to check on child marriage and sexual harassment cases. These surveys go on for 6 months prior to the start of new academic year. Each team of 5 to 6 members works on Sundays and covers upto 10 villages, working from 6 am to 10 pm. And this has yielded excellent results.

698 children have been admitted to school so far through the efforts of Bulland Udaan.

After admission, the group members continue to follow up with the family, neighbours and teachers numbers, to check that the child is actually attending. Due to which, there are very few dropouts.

But many challenges remain. When Bulland Udaan surveyed Badopal village, they found that the Bhaat community is not educating girls.

"If you want us to send girls to school will Bulland Udaan take responsibility that no girl will run away?" they ask. These are issues to which there is no easy solution…

Bulland Udaan is presently in Haryana working in 3 districts: Fatehabad, Hissar and Sirsa.

At present, Anju needs about Rs 7000 per month to carry on her work, and mostly, she is supported by her father, who is a man of modest means. Driving a truck to make a living.

"*Ab mere mummy-papa shaan se kehte hain - dekho hamari beti kya kaam kar rahi hai.*" (My parents are very proud of the work I am doing.)

Along with all her social work, Anju is also a serious student. She is currently in class 12, with physics, chemistry and biology as her subjects. With the goal of becoming a doctor. Anju wakes up early in the morning - as that, she feels - is the most productive time if one wants to study without any distraction.

"*Aagey bahut kuch karna hai... aur seekhna bhi hai* (There is a lot to do, and a lot to learn)."

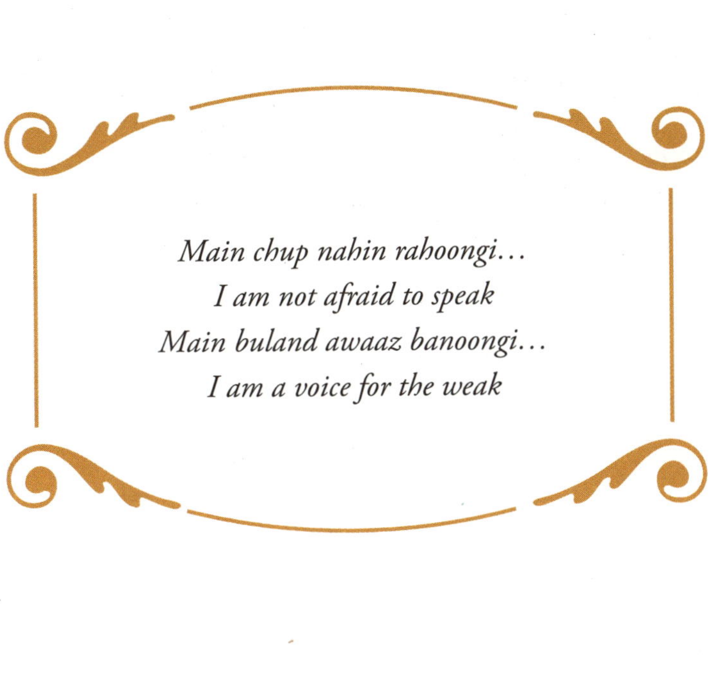

*Main chup nahin rahoongi…*
*I am not afraid to speak*
*Main buland awaaz banoongi…*
*I am a voice for the weak*

**MOHAMMAD HASNAIN LONE**

Age 16, Waragram (Kashmir)

# THE GOOD FIGHT

In the midst of conflict, a young boy is fighting for a different cause. The future of children and a drug-free Kashmir

In the troubled valley of Kashmir where normalcy is a luxury, Hasnain is eager to attend school.

"I live in a small village, we don't have a secondary sakool. I go to the government sakool in the next village, which is 2 kilometers away."

Come rain, shine or snow, Hasnain looks forward to attending classes. But while he is trying hard to pay attention to what the teacher is writing on the blackboard, most of the class is distracted. They have little or no interest in studies. And given the circumstances, you can't really blame them.

"*Yahaan ke haalaat bahut kharaab hain…* (the situation here is always tense)."

Waragram village looks like 'paradise on earth'. In summer, flowers are in bloom and the sun bounces off snow-capped mountains. In winter, the chinar trees stand tall and white, and Kashmiris go about their business with kangris* under their colourful firans.

"But one can never say… when something terrible can happen!"

---

* a personal heater (firepot) which keeps people warm

In the dead of the night, there is a knock on the door. It could be a fugitive, evading Indian military forces. It could be the army, in pursuit of such fugitives. There is senseless violence - people die on both sides. The Kashmiris are considered to be martyrs.

"There are many rallies and protests... one time, we refused to participate."

And so, the family became a target. Neighbours threw stones at them, and at their windows. When they refused to give in, a mob descended on the compound. Burning down their modest, wooden home. The family stood its ground and stayed in the same village.

"We have built a new house in the same compound... though it is still incomplete."

The cycle of peace, followed by unrest, continues unabated. When the situation gets bad, schools are the first to be shut. The shutdown could last a week, a month, or even longer*. Idle minds and idle hands are not easy for parents to handle.

---

* In 2017, government schools in Kashmir were open for only 90 days as against the required 170.

"*Is liye yahan ke bachche bigad rahe hain* (our children are getting attracted to wrong things)", says Hasnain's mother, Aamna Fatima.

In the village below Waragram, there are some people who consume and trade in drugs. They lure children and get them into the habit. Once addicted, the child begins stealing from his own home - or other homes - to buy his daily fix.

"This is one of the biggest problem in our village… which is ruining the lives of children I know!"

But what could 14 year old Hasnain do about it? Would those boys listen to him?

"*Haan, kyun nahin sunenge…*" said Aamna Fatima, always ready to support a good cause. Her desire to 'do something' for her village had taken her to a meeting held by an NGO*. Where she volunteered to become part of a 'Child Protection Committee'.

The same NGO was now conducting an awareness program among children themselves, in 10 villages of Budgam district.

---

* Save the Children, funded by Ikea Foundation

"You go there, and tell them about the problems your friends are facing," she advised Hasnain.

The meeting was held in an open ground next to the school, where boys played cricket and girls did hopscotch. But that afternoon was different. Sohail bhai explained to them 'what are child rights'. It was a new and exciting idea for all of them!

Hasnain started attending the monthly meetings, where slowly, children began opening up about various issues. Including the problem of drugs. At one such meeting, Hasnain spoke up and made a strong statement.

"*Badey log darte hain... woh kuch nahin karenge.*" (The elders are scared, they won't do anything.)

It was time for children themselves to do something. Seeing Hasnain's enthusiasm, Sohail bhai readily offered every possible support.

"*Yeh bahut acchhi baat hai...* but you have to be careful."

It would not be wise to take the people selling drugs head on.

"You children can take out a rally to create awareness about drug addiction," he advised.

And that's exactly what Hasnain did. He gathered the support of as many children as possible. But even he was surprised when, on the day of the rally, more than 350 boys and girls joined him. They marched through their own village and the village downhill, carrying placards and shouting slogans

"We want a future! We want a drug-free Kashmir!"

The rally got a wonderful response from villagers and sent out a strong message to dealers. But Hasnain did not stop there. He started visiting the homes of kids who were taking drugs, to inform their parents. Some of them refused to believe him.

"*Kya bakwas kar rahe ho*... you are talking nonsense about my son!" one father shouted at him.

But a few days later, he came to apologise, and thank Hasnain.

"You were right," he said. "My son is addicted to charas (cannabis). Tell me, what to do!"

"We believe that Kashmir will progress when children are educated, as there is a tendency nowadays to use children wherever there is an opportunity to make money."

It is not easy to get these children to kick the habit. Some of them are able to stop, when they face the wrath of parents. Others need medical help, for which they must go to a de-addiction centre.

"We also need more support from the government, from the police..."

There have been cases where the village committee has gone so far as asking a drug dealer to leave the village. But the police force is lax and does not take strict action. People have told Aamna and her husband to keep their son away from such people.

**At the end of the day, drugs are a symptom of a much deeper problem.**

"They told me not to speak against drugs... but I am not afraid. I will continue to raise my voice!"

At the end of the day, drugs are a symptom of a much deeper problem. Many parents would rather send their children to work, rather than school. The boys collect firewood in the jungle or tend sheep while the girls sew carpets. Many of these girls start sniffing tobacco or using hookah.

"Because they have no future, nothing to look forward to."

Hasnain and the other children in his group visit the homes of such children and convince their parents to do the right thing. After all, everything is being provided free of cost - books, uniform, even food. Thanks to these efforts, 3 child labourers are now enrolled in school.

"In my free time, I give tuitions to those children who cannot afford it..."

Hasnain and his two younger sisters have the love and support of their parents. But every child is not as lucky. Many parents scold and beat their kids, which only alienates them. And creates an easy target for anti-social elements.

"*Bachche ko pyaar se hi samjhana chahiye*... children respond only when spoken to, with love."

A man in the village used to berate his son all the time, for small things. The son was always sad and depressed. Hasnain decided to speak to the father.

"If you shout at your son, it is of no use... he will only become more stubborn."

The father realised his folly and became more understanding. The boy became more responsible.

That night, Hasnain went to bed with peace in his heart, for his efforts are making a difference. Despite all obstacles, he is determined to continue.

*And while politicians continue their fights,*
*on the television debates nightly.*
*In one little village of Kashmir, the lamp*
*of love glows. A little more brightly.*

**JHULIMA MALLICK**

Age 22, Bandudi (Odisha)

# FLAME OF THE FOREST

A tribal girl gets inspired to work for her community. Bringing better health and education to a remote part of Odisha.

Jhulima grew up in a tiny village at the foothill of a dense forest.

"I hail from the Kondh tribe hence the area we live in is known as Kandhamal."

For thousands of years, the Kondhs have lived in harmony with nature. Mothers carry their infants into the forest while collecting firewood. They weave leaves from the Sal tree into plates and cups. And they cultivate high-quality organic turmeric. However, they do not get a fair price for their labour.

Most households in this remote area are below the poverty line. Yet, they are a little better off than their counterparts in other parts of the country. In Kandhamal, no family sells their girl for Rs 500 - so they can buy liquor. All they have to do is tap the toddy tree for alcohol, whenever they want it.

"Nature has given us everything… but we lack facilities of education and health."

The government has set up residential schools for tribal boys and girls. Jhulima was enrolled in one such school but she had to leave the hostel when she fell sick. She then stayed with her mama (maternal uncle) and here, she had to cross a river to reach her school each day.

One morning, after heavy rain, the river was in spate. Yet Jhulima, and 6 other girls, bravely set off for school. As they made the crossing, the water level kept rising. Teachers on the other side were frantically waving out - warning them to turn back. Finally, the girls realised there was no choice.

"That day I realised how important school was for me… I wasn't willing to miss a single day, if I could help it!"

Not an easy ambition for a tribal girl. For soon after she hit puberty, Jhulima got a proposal for marriage. She was a student of class 7 at the time. Nothing out of the ordinary in Odisha, where 21.8% girls are married before the age of 18 (officially). The actual numbers are far higher…

In the past, there was no concept of 'marriage' among the Kondhs. In the month of April, during the 'Dand Yatra'*, a 15 year old boy and 14 year old girl may see each other, like each other and simply elope. Tribal customs are now

---

* during this festival a moorti (stone likeness) of Lord Shiva is taken from village to village.

less prevalent but parents remain keen to marry off their daughters as early as possible.

Yet, Jhulima stood up to the pressure from her family and refused.

"The groom's family said we are willing to wait… but I told them 'no' and continued my education."

Unfortunately, Jhulima was unable to complete her class 10 board exams. At the time, her mother was unwell and admitted to the District Headquarter Hospital in Phulbani. So the family was under severe financial stress. She could not afford to fill out the form and had no choice but to drop out.

Life was looking quite bleak for Jhulima until, in 2016, she met the anganwadi didi in her village and learnt about an NGO called SWATI*.

"They are conducting a training program for girls like you… would you like to join?"

Jhulima didn't know exactly what this meant but she was curious. Besides, didi had promised there would be free

---

* Social Welfare and Training Institute (SWATI), local partner of Save the Children

food and stay. So, along with a friend, Jhulima decided to attend the program. The two girls set out on foot, and walked the entire 12 kms from Bandudi to the venue in Bandaguda.

On the first day, Jhulima sat silently, feeling a little lost and out-of-place. She did have things to say but was afraid - what if someone laughed at her? The trainer spoke about the importance of nutrition - what one should eat. They also talked about child marriage and its ill-effects.

"I could immediately relate to this... as it almost happened to me. What I learnt here was that child marriage is also against the law*."

Slowly, Jhulima became more confident and started participating in discussions. But what she enjoyed the most was performing in the skit. Every evening, the girls would enact something they had learnt in the course of the day. One would play the role of the mother, another of a father, and so on.

Jhulima discovered that she had a natural talent for acting. Though tiny in size, she had a powerful persona on stage.

---

* Rs 1 lakh fine and 1 year imprisonment to anyone abetting child marriage

And when she returned to Banduda after the 5-day training program, she knew one thing: 'I must share what I have learnt with others'. And the ideal medium to do this was the street play.

"When we performed in the village, some people praised the effort while others made fun of us… but we didn't feel bad about that!"

Jhulima went on to form a girls group which goes from village to village, performing street plays. The aim is to spread awareness and prevent early marriages.

And the effort had made solid impact. A young girl called Kesari had received a proposal for marriage on the very same day that she saw the play. She actually went home and refused, saying that it is wrong and illegal to marry before the age of 18. Over the last 2 years, Jhulima's efforts have prevented more than 12 such child marriages.

"I work with different officials at village, Gram Panchayat, block and district level… in an extreme case, we have even had to file an FIR."

It is indeed not easy to challenge age-old beliefs. Jhulima recalls the time she was distributing leaflets in a

"I told all my friends that iron is good for you - I have these tablets daily and so must you!"

हमारा साथ, हमारा स्वास्थ्य
PARTNERS'

**That day I realised how important school was for me.**

neighbouring village and came to know of an under-age couple who were to be married. She called Childline and thus prevented the marriage from taking place. The two families threatened her with dire consequences, but Jhulima took it in her stride.

"I know I am doing good work, so why should I get scared?" was her response.

Health is another issue close to Jhulima's heart. One of the major problems in K-Nuagaon block is the high prevalence of malaria. Hence, Jhulima took the lead in the MDD-MR (Malaria, Dengue, Diarrhoea-Measles, Rubella) campaign held in her area. The adolescent girls of the community also worked together to implement Swachcha Bharat Abhiyan.

Alongside, Jhulima made efforts to educate girls about the benefits of iron tablets. These tablets are distributed free of cost from the government's anganwadi centre, every Saturday. But they had no takers. Some girls felt dizzy after consuming the tablet and there were many misconceptions about it. Jhulima cleared their doubts and confusion.

"I told all my friends that iron is good for you - I have these tablets daily and so must you!"

Indeed, there is no shortage of schemes from the government. What we need is champions who work from within, and get the community to adopt them.

It is therefore heartening that Jhulima has been selected as President of Block Level Girls' Federation in K.Nuagaon block of Kandhamal district, representing 2000 girls of her age. In addition, she recently received the V-Award from the United Nations for her efforts to bring change in her community.

And though she works in many areas, Jhulima's first love remains education. She was able to counsel 3 girls who had dropped out of school to re-enrol themselves. And she has also been instrumental in motivating 6 girls to join the Skill Development Training* program offered by the state government.

"In fact, I was also very excited about being a part of this program but sadly, I could not complete it..."

---

* under Deen Dayal Upadhyaya Grameen Kaushal Yojana (DDU-GKY)

This was due to the sudden demise of her father in February 2018. Jhulima had no choice but to return home and supplement her family's meagre income by working as a daily wage labourer under NREGA. At the same time she is happy that one of the girls who did complete the training is now employed in Chennai at a salary of Rs 8000 per month.

And she remains hopeful about her future. Recently, with the help of SWATI, she joined the National Open School (NIOS) and plans to enrol for college after passing class 10.

"I would also like to work in Chennai or Bangalore… and also do social work."

Jhulima is part of a new tribe, a tribe of changemakers.

*We are children of the forest,*
*children of the trees*
*We welcome winds of change,*
*the pleasant new breeze*

SHAILENDRA SINGH
Age 19, Tonk (Rajasthan)

# THE RIGHT STUFF

Social work is his calling. Shunning a life of ease and privilege, Shailendra takes up the cause of child rights for the less fortunate.

Shailendra is one of those rare young men who has everything but wants to do something for others.

"My grandfather was a village sarpanch (headman)… *main bhi unki tarah gaon ke liye kuch karna chahta hoon* (I too want to serve the people)."

The problems in this part of the world are aplenty. Tonk district in Rajasthan state has neither tourism nor industry. It has substantial Muslim population with large family size. Most families eke out a living rolling tendu patta into beedis (local cigarettes). For 1000 beedis, the tobacco company pays a meagre Rs 100.

"The women do this work from home… even children join in after school. They are not really encouraged to study."

*Padh likh kar kya kar loge* (What's your future even after schooling) is a common opinion. And that's true even for the boys. With hardly any jobs available, there is no incentive to study beyond class 10 or 12. In any case, the government schools are hardly imparting any real education.

"Even after going to school most of the children cannot read or do *hisaab* (addition)."

If you don't stop I will be forced to make a video and send it to our sir in the NGO.

The single-room, single-teacher school is common and it's normal to hit students for disobedience… or just because the teacher is having a bad day. This used to bother Shailendra but he had no idea what he could do about it. Even if an injustice was happening right in front of his own eyes.

"*Bura lagta tha lekin kuch kehne ki meri himmat nahi thi* (I felt bad but did not have courage to protest)."

Well, someone up there heard Shailendra's silent prayers. When he was only 8 years old a Bal Samooh (children's group) was set up in his village. Here, for the first time, Shailendra became aware of many new ideas which came under the umbrella of 'child rights'.

For example, 'good touch' and 'bad touch' was taught to kids, through the medium of a game. Later, Shailendra joined the Kishore Samooh (youth group) where he enjoyed the Lalita and Babu training module. Finally, he felt empowered to 'do something'! Instead of playing cricket, he started attending the Sunday morning meeting of the samooh.

"We were 20–25 kids and divided up the work amongst ourselves… to identify various problems children face."

The tasks included making a list of kids who have dropped out of school. And then find a way to re-enrol them.

Another issue the group took up is that of children with disabilities. These kids are entitled to a pension from the state but are unaware of the fact. So, it is the Kishore Samooh which took the responsibility of making a list of eligible recipients from each village. Many do not have the required disability certificate.

"We get the certificates made and then apply for the pension through the E-mitra portal of Rajasthan government."

Sometimes, there is an administrative lapse due to which pension is still not sanctioned. In which case the samooh speaks to its mentor to solve the problem. Thanks to these efforts, around 20 disabled children have started receiving monetary benefits. They are not just from Shailendra's village, but from the neighbouring 4–5 panchayats.

The spark of leadership did not go unnoticed. Shailendra was appointed to the District-level Child Protection Committee (DCPC) and this energised him even further. A disabled woman in his neighbourhood was being beaten by her husband. Shailendra went to meet him and urged him to stop.

"*Kya samajhta hai apne aap ko yeh chhokra* (who does this boy think he is)?" screamed the husband.

Shailendra remained calm. He said, "If you don't stop I will be forced to make a video and send it to our sir in the NGO."

The man complained to Shailendra's father. But received no support.

"If you do something wrong... I can't stop Shailendra from complaining," said pappa.

And, scared of the outcome, the man gave up beating his wife. Many such cases keep coming to Shailendra's notice.

"We intervene to stop domestic violence because it has a very bad effect on children."

Wife-beating usually occurs under the influence of alcohol. So, the Kishore Samooh decided to address this aspect as well. A *sharaab ka theka* (liquor store) had been set up in Shailendra's village. In actual fact, the owner did not have the permission to do so. But in the past people did, and got away with it.

This time was different. Shailendra and his friends went door-to-door, collecting signatures on a petition. While some men refused to sign, their wives and children did. The village sarpanch and panchayat members also supported the effort. It was collectively agreed that anyone who sells liquor without license will be fined Rs 11,000.

"The theka was shut down and it is a positive thing for the entire community."

Coming to child marriage - one of the most detrimental social customs in Tonk. Due to growing awareness, the practice has reduced to an extent. But it also gone underground. All the group members are therefore instructed to keep their eyes and ears open. Because there are tell-tale signs. Such as a house getting painted around the time of *dev uthaoni*.*

---

* the auspicious period in the Hindu calendar when weddings can take place

"I am prepared to fight till no kid is deprived of his or her childhood. I don't care if it takes all my life to achieve this."

"*Agar hamein pata chal jaaye to kisi bhi keemat par hum shaadi rukwa dete hain.*" (Once we suspect a child marriage is taking place we stop it no matter what the cost.)

This was not always easy to do. Because if and when someone complained to the local police, they would come and 'stop' the wedding. But it was all *jhooth mooth* (fake). In actual fact, the policeman might demand a bribe and let the wedding take place. The person who complained was branded a 'troublemaker' and could even get beaten up!

All this has changed due to the 1098 helpline number. When anyone calls this number, his or her identity is not revealed. The police now comes to the venue with an NGO worker.

So no 'setting' is possible. And no child marriage either.

While policing and protecting is very important, real change is more subtle, more lasting. And it is now visible. Shailendra recalls that just a few years ago, when a lady in his neighbourhood had 3 daughters in a row, there was a pall of gloom. People offered her condolences.

"*Aapke karam achche nahin honge*.... (you are cursed by fate)," they said to her.

Now, when someone has a second daughter, there are celebrations in that home.

"*Tumhare ghar to Lachchmi hui hai.*" (Goddess Lakshmi has come to your house.)

Shailendra was recently nominated for the International Children's Peace Prize. And that only strengthened his resolve to work in this field.

His dream is that all children should have the right to decide their path in life. Without any *jor zabardasti* (undue pressure). And certainly, Shailendra knows what he wants. When Shailendra's father wanted to send him to Sikar to join a 'good private school', he refused. It was not his desire to study science or become a 'topper' like his elder brother.

"I want to pursue a Master's in Social Work and set up my own NGO. Bhaiyya* has supported me... I know I will achieve my goal."

---

* elder brother

In fact, Shailendra plans to work in Ajmer district, which is even more backward than Tonk.

And desperately needs nayi soch (new thinking). Along naya josh (new energy).

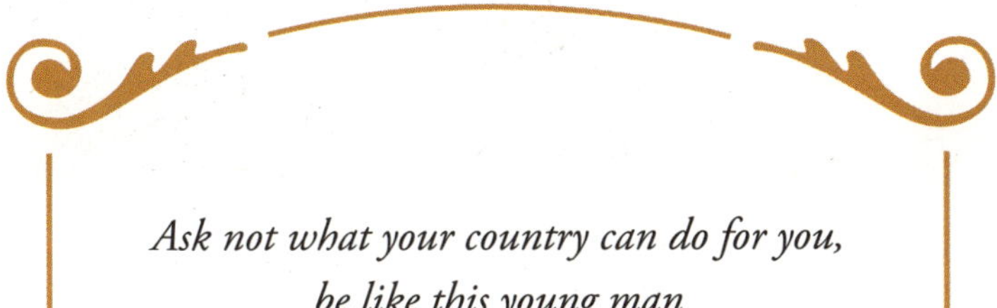

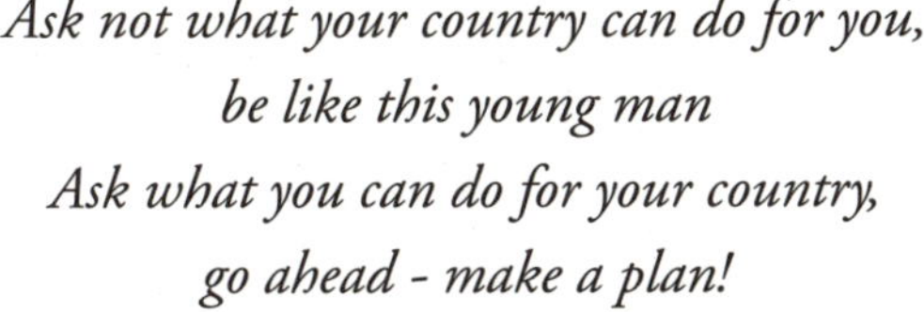

*Ask not what your country can do for you,*
*be like this young man*
*Ask what you can do for your country,*
*go ahead - make a plan!*

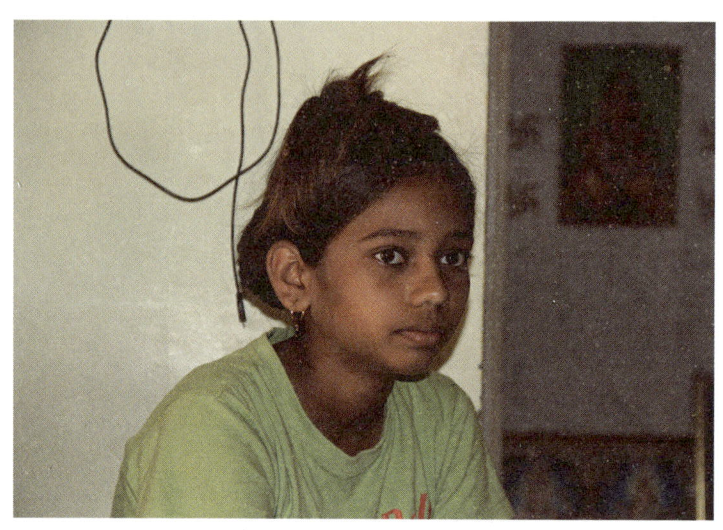

**KALAVATHI V.A.**

Age 15, Kurubarahalli (Karnataka)

# CLEAN SWEEP

As 'Prime Minister' of the school cabinet, Kalavathi works for the welfare of her fellow students.

Kalavathi was one of the lucky girls whose parents willingly and eagerly sent her to school.

"Not only me but my 2 elder sisters also went to school… amma and appa always supported."

Kalavathi's father makes a living selling nuts on the street in Hospet city in north Karnataka; her mother is a labourer. But they sensed that education was the way forward for their daughters.

But at the age of 12, Kalavathi was on the verge of leaving school. Every afternoon, she came home with a sad face. And she was always looking for excuses to bunk classes.

"My stomach is paining today, amma, " she would say, making all the right noises to convince her. But mothers are not easily fooled. Reluctantly, Kalavathi set out for school.

So what was the real problem? Well, school was around 10 kilometres away and there was no bus plying that route. Neither could she afford to take an auto rickshaw daily. So, Kalavathi had to walk to school and back - a difficult and tiring journey. Even that would have been okay… but what to do about those rakshasas on the way?

These demons were boys in 9th and 10th class, with leery eyes and thin whiskery moustaches. At first they just stared, making her uncomfortable. But soon they became bolder.

"They would start whistling or singing some film songs…. I felt very embarrassed and scared!"

And how could she talk about this with her parents? They might think she was to blame! So Kalavathi started thinking, it might be best to just drop out of school….

Well, somehow the year passed. Kalavathi joined class 7. And one afternoon, she was told to stay back in school by her teacher.

"You are selected to attend a special program," teacher had said.

The program was Samudaya Abhiruddhi* and it was so interesting! A kindly didi in a pretty salwar kameez talked

---

* this program was facilitated by Save the Children

about the importance of personal hygiene. Why, she even talked about how to keep one's toilet clean! Kalavathi's mind went to the stinky washroom in her own school (which she hated to use).

"Oh, our school toilet should sparkle like that!" she thought to herself.

**One has to speak up, get support of others and find solutions.**

There was a video presentation which laid out the '6 steps of personal hygiene'. Kalavathi took copious notes. That evening she skipped her way home, ignoring the ruffians on the way.

"We must all wash our hands before our meals," she said to her family that night.

And she eagerly shared what she had learnt with classmates and neighbours. Seeing this enthusiasm, Kalavathi's teacher inducted her into the school cabinet.

At the very first meeting, Kalavathi was nervous. But it was not like a regular classroom where the teacher spoke and students listened. Each and every child present was asked to speak, to share any problem he or she was facing. Slowly, Kalavathi felt confident enough to talk about her own problem while coming and going to school.

To her surprise, there were other girls facing the same issue!

"We decided that there is strength in numbers, so we should all walk together and scold those boys, if they misbehave."

Problems *can* be overcome, Kalavathi realised. One has to speak up, get support of others and find solutions. Her mind once again went to the dirty school toilet.

"Can't we do something about it?" she asked in the weekly school cabinet meeting.

Manjunath Sir liked the idea and decided to form a WASH (Water, Sanitation and Hygiene) committee to tackle the matter.

The problem was quite simple - the entire school had only one sweeper. She could not cope up with the workload. So it was decided to form 4-5 teams consisting of children. Each day one team would assist the sweeper in cleaning the classrooms and if necessary, even toilets. The headmaster gladly provided additional buckets and brooms.

"Even some of the teachers joined in… because this is *our* school… let it be as clean as home."

In no time, the Vemgal government school building and its toilets became spick and span. A model for other schools to emulate! This was followed up by a campaign to make the school plastic-free. Many children had the habit of eating sweets and carelessly throwing the wrappers around. They were strictly monitored by the students and made to use the dustbin.

Lack of drinking water was another problem faced by the students. This was brought to the notice of the headmaster. The WASH committee also monitored the cleaning of the water tank.

Many children complained that their shoes got wet while using the toilets.

"We spoke to our headmaster and he agreed to provide slippers."

"I want to educate myself very well...then, from my earnings I can give some money to those who don't have enough for their education."

In the summer vacation, Kalavathi attended a summer camp*. On the last 2 days, the children went to a village called Purahalli and conducted a door-to-door survey.

"What problems do you face?" they asked. "Do you have running water, do you have a toilet?"

After taking note of all the points, a meeting was called with the panchayat member and BDO (Block Development Officer). They promised to address all the issues.

During her Dussehra holidays, Kalavathi decided to conduct the same survey in another village, with the help of her friends. Once again, they met the gram panchayat members to share the findings. And continued to follow up. In a few short months, there was *visible* change. Better roads, more street lights... And slowly but steadily, a leader was born.

In class 8, Kalavathi was elected as 'Prime Minister' of the school cabinet. She presides over the meetings with a friendly but firm air. But it is not enough to merely discuss, *action* must be taken.

---

* also by Save the Children

In 2018, Kalavathi was actively involved in the framing of Children's Manifesto* which outlined the demands of children to the political parties preparing to fight state assembly elections.

"We need basic facilities, such as good transport to go to school," said Kalavathi, speaking confidently and eloquently at a function organised at the Bangalore press club. The presence of government officials, media and even film stars such as Sri Murali did not faze her. For where there is purpose, strength will follow…

"It is her character - to help, support and take care of others," say her teachers.

Little wonder then that Kalavathi was selected as the recipient of the 'Changemaker' award instituted at Mount Carmel college.

At age 14, Kalavathi knows what she wants to do in life.

"I want to educate very well… so I can help people to 'develop their life'…"

---

* a charter of demands prepared by children, given to major political parties before the general election 2019

Perhaps as a teacher, or a social worker, a doctor, or a government officer. Who knows? But of this one thing there is no doubt… we need more Kalavathis.

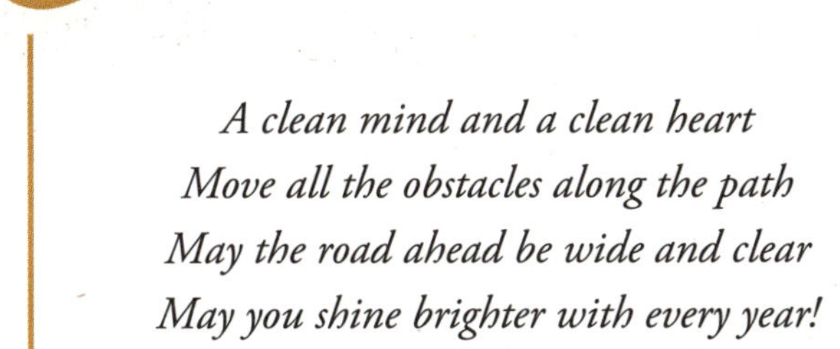

*A clean mind and a clean heart*
*Move all the obstacles along the path*
*May the road ahead be wide and clear*
*May you shine brighter with every year!*

**SUJANTI KUMARI**

Age 23, Gaya (Bihar)

# THE PRICE IS NOT RIGHT

The practice of giving dowry destroys lives. Sujanti Kumari has raised her melodious voice against this evil.

Growing up in rural Bihar, Sujanti Kumari was often troubled by the 'way things are' and poured her thoughts and feelings into her school notebook.

"I used to show my jottings to my elder sister… who would laugh and say *ki duniya aisi hi hai.*" (The world will stay as it is.)

But in her own small way, she too, was fighting back. Their father was not very keen to send his daughters to school. His logic was '*saadi hi to karni hai*' (they will only get married).

"It's like throwing your money into the well," he would say.

And money was already scarce. When it rained, the family would stay up all night to collect water leaking through the tin roof. There was just about enough to eat and no savings to fall back on.

"We didn't have proper clothes to wear but still my sister and I used to think *ki kisi tarah padh lein, kuch lar lein* (somehow we must study and achieve something)."

The girls did manual labour during the rice harvest season and got paid in the form of grain. But that was not of much use when it came to paying fees. Luckily, Sujanti's sister got a job with a local NGO called Mahila Samakhya, earning a modest salary of Rs 1000 per month. So she was able to complete Inter (class 12).

But soon after that, she was married and with that, came a new problem. The burden of debt.

"*Ladki ki saadi* (the wedding of a daughter) means the groom's family must receive dowry in cash and kind. That is the custom everyone follows."

The girl's family will beg, borrow and blow up a lifetime of precious capital, to show a fine face to the world, for a single day. Sujanti's father did what he had to.

"*Ab tum bhi padhaai chhod do* (now you also don't waste time on education)," he said to his younger daughter. But she rebelled against the diktat.

"I used to cry a lot and I insisted I will study," Sujanti recalls.

In this endeavour, her mother was a silent supporter. Her meagre earnings as a street vendor were spent towards Sujanti's schooling. And thus was she able to pass Matric (class 10) with 2nd division. With new found confidence and a sense of purpose, Sujanti started giving tuitions to a few children at home, for Rs 50 a month. And she passed the Inter (class 12 exam) with 1st division.

*Par aagey padhaai kaise hogi* (how will I go to college?) was the question in her mind.

Since childhood, Sujanti was fond of singing and dancing. Her melodious voice was much appreciated by all. So as luck would have it, a 'sir' from a private school nearby asked her to come and train his kids for the annual day function. That was a job Sujanti really enjoyed. And with the money it brought in, she was able to enrol for BA part 1.

Around the same time, her elder brother got married. He received a dowry of Rs 90,000 in cash. But it was a short-lived windfall. A good proposal had come for Sujanti and it was quickly accepted.

"The dowry my brother had brought was given to my in-laws - Rs 50, 000 in cash and a motorbike."

Sujanti and her husband barely spent 15 days together, when he hurried off to distant Gujarat, to take up a job in a factory. He didn't have a choice. The family was also reeling under the burden of debt – money borrowed at exorbitant interest rates from the village mahajan to marry his sister with an adequate dowry.

And so it goes, and so it goes.

**For the good of life, it would be better to be unmarried.**

Sujanti has a younger sister and her marriage is looming large. *Kahaan se aayega paisa*? (Where will the money come from?)

"Seeing my own family and my sasural (husband's family), I strongly feel this practice of dowry must end!"

While Sujanti completes her education, she is also an active member of the Children's Groups Alumni network*. This voluntary work serves as an outlet for her anger and frustration against the ills of society. Poured out in the form of drama and song. These are her mediums of choice when trying to spread the important message: '*Na dahej lena hai, na dahej dena hai*'. (Let us pledge to neither give nor take dowry.)

"The young people listen and they agree... but the elders continue the practice," she says. Still, they do stop and

* formed by Samagra Seva Kendra, Save the Children's local partner, to harness skills of Child Champions, after they reach adulthood

listen spellbound when she breaks into a passionate song about the horrors of *dahej pratha* (the custom of dowry). Which pierces the heart, even after being translated from Bhojpuri into English*.

*If I would have known that you will be burnt in fire of dowry,*
*I never would have committed such a sin of sending you to in-laws.*

O dear, you have suffered a lot of deep distress and you might have spent your days and night in sorrow.

Sobbing with deep pain in the heart sounding (maa-maa.)

*If I would have known that you will be burnt in fire of dowry,*
*I never would have committed such a sin of sending you to in-laws.*

O daughter! What can I say about my fate…

Why you would you come to a poor man's house as a daughter

I should have not let you marry, rather kept you unmarried.
We would have heard abuse (gaali) of people
I would have never separated a piece of my heart.

---

* the Bhojpuri song is titled *'janti ki jaaral jaibu'*

Save the Children
Breaking barriers to achieve res
Training of
Adolescents Se
Health
Date :-
Place :-

"Through the trainings I am doing etc., I want to encourage and empower girls who may be in tight situations like me, to struggle hard and break through all the challenges."

*If I would have known that you will be burnt in fire of dowry, I never would have committed such a sin of sending you to in-laws.*

How vulgar are the customs of society

Giving poison while pretending with love

For the good of life, it would be better to be unmarried.

*If I would have known that you will be burnt in fire of dowry, I never would have committed such a sin of sending you to in-laws.*

But what of those who knowingly, or unknowingly, continue to commit this sin, just so they can say 'my daughter is married'. When will this suffering end?

"I hope that someday our government imposes harsh penalties on all those who give and take dowry," says Sujanti. "Just like they did for child marriage".

Until then, she will continue to raise her melodious voice against injustice.

*For there can be no MRP (Minimum Retail Price)*
*for a human being. A bride.*
*That is the India of my dreams.*
*Where girls live with dignity, and pride.*

PADHENGE
We Will Learn

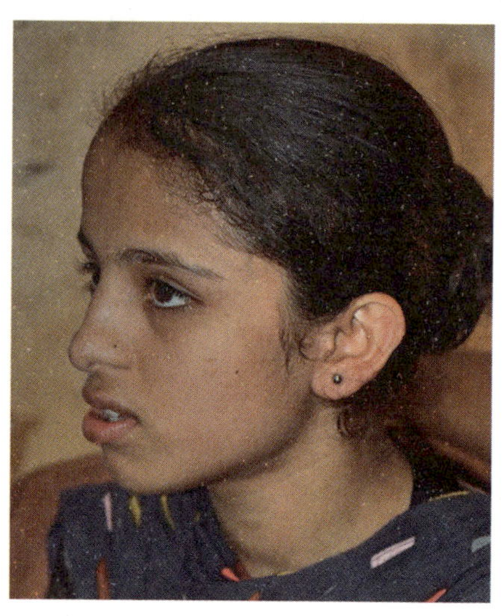

**SALEHA KHAN**

Age 20, Govandi (Mumbai)

# A SPRING IN HER STEP

Her father didn't want her to study after class 8. But with quiet determination she got her way, and paved the way for other girls.

Saleha grew up in Govandi, a part of Mumbai where humans co-exist with flies, filth and faeces.

"My father has a cycle repair shop, my mother is a housewife... we are originally from U.P."

This is an area which the town - and its planners - has conveniently forgotten. For its residents are low-income, migrant families. And by the way, we need to dump our garbage somewhere... so let's do it here. That dumping ground has grown and grown into what is, literally, a mountain of filth. Saleha recalls playing in the dumping ground, as a child.

"We didn't know it was a dirty place... my friends used to climb up and down the heaps of garbage and pick up expired bags of chips."

Once Saleha's mother caught her with one such packet and snatched it from her, with a scolding. She warned the little girl not to go there and that eating such things would make her sick.

"Don't go there again," she warned. "*Bachchon ke liye theek nahi hai*". (It's not good for children.)

But where else could the children jump and run around? Like any other slum in Mumbai (but a few degrees worse!) Bainganwadi was cramped and overcowded, with narrow lanes and overflowing gutters. Why, quite often, the gutter water flowed right into Saleha's tiny one-room house which she shared with 6 family members.

"It was difficult… there was no toilet in our home, or even a water connection."

The slum-dwellers had to buy water from tankers, at a cost of Rs 30 to Rs 50 per gallon. The buckets would have to be hauled back to the home over quite a distance. Everyone was surprised to see Saleha - with her small build - helping her mother with this daily chore. And, she always did it with a smile.

"*Bachpan se hi Saleha ka bahut helping nature hai*," says her mother. (From childhood, Saleha has the desire to be of help to others.)

Unlike most girls of her age, Saleha was also very keen to attend school. The government school in Govandi is only upto class 7. The secondary school is in Chembur, which is quite some distance away. Saleha's father was not keen to send her there. He had never been to school himself and didn't really see the value of education.

"*Hamesha padhti rahegi kya*?" (What's the point of studying all the time?)

Saleha's elder sister had already dropped out of school, she stayed home helping out their mother. It took quite a bit of convincing for abbu (father) to relent. The local school teacher came to their home and counselled him, as well. Finally, it was Saleha who came up with a workable plan. She convinced 3 other girls from the neighbourhood to join the same school.

"We will all travel together - *ek doosre ka khayal rakhenge*!" (We will keep each other safe.)

Although soft-spoken and respectful, Saleha has always had a mind of her own.

One morning, social workers from the NGO Apnalaya had come to her home, to inform them about menstrual hygiene classes. Saleha's mother forbade her from joining.

She thought her daughter - the age 12 - was 'too young' for this adult information. After all young girls get all kinds of ideas and are often led astray…

**Although soft-spoken, Saleha has always had a mind of her own.**

Although her mother did not grant permission, Saleha decided to go anyway. And she found the class very useful and interesting. The instructor explained what is menstruation, how to use a pad, how to maintain hygiene during periods. And it was all done in the form of discussion and games.

"*Class mein achcha achcha batate hain,*" she told her mother. (They teach us positive things.)

In fact, after about a year, Saleha felt she knew enough to take a class herself. Though a bit nervous in the beginning, she found her confidence.

"I felt really happy when girls came and told me these classes were helping them!"

After scoring 59% in the 10th board exams, Saleha was able to join a junior college closer to home, along with her friends. Meanwhile, she got an opportunity to take self defence training through an NGO called Aangan. They taught girls how to face attackers by using martial arts and even chilli powder!

"*Kabhi real mein use kiya nahi* (Never had to use it in real life) but I felt I can face any situation!"

It was around this time that Saleha's small acts of courage came to the notice of the Sakaal newspaper group, which has instituted the Savitribai Phule award. This award is usally given to an older woman working towards a social cause. But they were so impressed by 17-year-old Saleha, that they shortlisted her name.

For the very first time, her humble household was visited by a journalist. Who went back satisfied *ki story mein dum hai* (it's a true and inspiring story).

The award ceremony was held on 1st January, 2017 and the organisers had just one request.

"Please bring your father with you to attend the function in Ulhasnagar (a suburb of Mumbai)."

"Sometimes parents shut their doors when we go to meet them but we keep following up until they agree to hear us out."

After a great deal of persuasion, Shakil Khan agreed to accompany his daughter. He was astounded to see a huge crowd at the venue. And they were all clapping and cheering for Saleha.

"*Aaj mujhe bahut khushi hai* (I am very happy today)," he said. "You are no less than a boy for me."

This event became a turning point. Saleha's father now became her biggest supporter. When she completed her 12th and wanted to join a commerce college in Sanpada, which was at quite a distance from their home, he did not scold her, or raise any objection. In fact, he willingly bears as much expense as he possibly can, the rest is covered by a fellowship from the NGO Apnalaya.

Along with her studies, Saleha continues to take sessions on menstrual hygiene for girls (she has completed over 250 so far!). She also undertook a unique project to highlight the poor level of sanitation in the slum. Having learnt photography at a workshop organised by Save the Children, she decided to put this skill to good use.

"We took photographs of our area... the toilets, the garbage.. and organised an exhibition."

Filthy latrines, piles of muck and buzzing flies were indeed a common sight. But the residents had grown immune to it. But seeing those images blown up in full colour, HD, stirred something inside them. Women decided to monitor the hygiene in the common toilets and make sure they were cleaned at least twice a day. And slowly, there was visible change.

Things have improved for Saleha Khan and her family. She now lives in a 3-room vertical house with running water. The gutter outside her house has been fixed, and here too she has played a role. By persuading her mother and other women in the neighbourhood to sign a petition and deliver it to the local MLA.

"*Humne apna haq maanga aur wo humein mil gaya.*" (We demanded what was our right and got it.)

Fighting these battles is not easy - and more so for a young girl. Platforms like Ashoka Youth Venture played a role in building Saleha's confidence. When she attended the training session in Bangalore in 2017, she realised that there were so many other girls from all over India who had faced issues related to education, just like she had.

"Meeting these girls gave me strength… I thought I must be active and do good for others."

In September 2018, Saleha Khan was chosen as a #GirlChampion, who would speak on behalf of the girls of India, at the United Nations General Assembly session. As she boarded the Air India flight to New York City, she was both excited and nervous. It was her first time on an airplane and her first time in a foreign country.

At the forum, Saleha participated in discussions on 'Sustainable Development Goals'. She was thrilled to meet children like herself, from 155 countries. A film on education of the girl child was shown, in which Saleha's struggle was covered. When Melinda Gates spoke, she specifically mentioned the brave young girl from Mumbai. But she couldn't pronounce Saleha's name correctly.

"So after her speech I went and introduced myself… that I am Saleha, not Sally."

"Oh… I apologise for that," said Melinda Gates. "I am so happy to meet you in person."

Saleha returned to Mumbai energised and determined to 'do more'. One of the things she resolved to do was 'improve her English'. This would also help in her goal of doing a Master's in Social Work in Tata Institute of Social Sciences (TISS). Meanwhile, she continues to juggle her final year in college with giving tuitions to earn some extra income. And working with Apnalaya.

Saleha is a mentor for 14 girls in her community. She has the quiet credibility and authority to counsel parents to do what's right for their daughters. Let them go to school, not hurry to get them married. Not go through the trauma faced by her own sister - who had a baby at 16. Because she didn't know any better back then.

"*Ab to mere pappa bhi kehte hain… galti ho gayi, phir aisa nahin honey denge.*" (Even my father agrees, what happened with my sister was wrong and it should not happen again.)

This is change. Real and sustainable change. Change from within the community.

Going a step further, Saleha's mother adds, "If we keep our girls in purdah and let the boys roam around freely without any checks, that is not right either."

Both boys and girls must be sensitised on how to deal with their bodies, and with each other. So, these days *ladkon ki training bhi hoti hai* (there is training for boys too). The girls use a 'Paro' kit while the boys use 'Shankar' kit. When they recently interacted with celebrity Twinkle Khanna, both genders were present. And no one was embarrassed to talk about periods.

"*Bahut acchha lagta hai…*" Saleha beams. (It's wonderful to see this.)

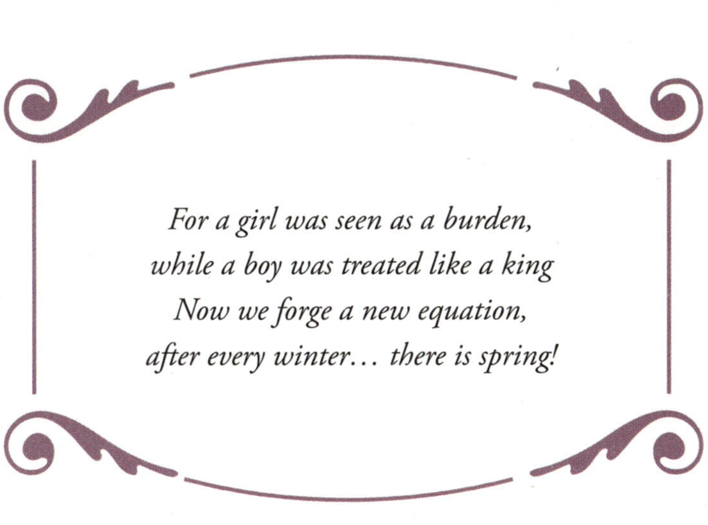

*For a girl was seen as a burden,*
*while a boy was treated like a king*
*Now we forge a new equation,*
*after every winter… there is spring!*

**SUBHDEEP KAUR**

Age 15, Jhandawala (Punjab)

# PICKING A NEW PATH

She toiled in the cotton fields of Punjab as a child. Now she thrives in school and is a role model in her district.

Subhdeep was born in Punjab - the land of 5 rivers - to a family which did not own any land.

"I was 7 or 8 years old when my mother started taking me to do *narma chugai* (cotton-picking)…."

The cotton-picking season in north India lasts from October to December each year. And it is difficult, back-breaking work. The delicate cotton flower must be picked carefully, an activity that takes intense effort. Workers stand in the field all day long, under the hot sun, with barely an hour of rest.

"At the end of the day my feet used to hurt and my fingers had blisters!"

If she was lucky, Subhdeep would manage to pick about 10 kg of cotton in a day, for which she was paid Rs 50. On some days, her employer would offer something to eat but only after deducting a few rupees from the daily wage. Bullying the workers and shouting at them for 'not working hard enough' was a daily occurrence.

One morning, Subhdeep was working in the field when she noticed a large, black snake, just a few metres away. The little girl froze in terror, not knowing what might happen next.... Then, the survival instinct kicked in and she ran as fast as she could! It was a few days before Subhdeep gathered the courage to return. But return she did.

"I did not like doing this work.... but I had no choice."

**I did not like doing this work.... but I had no choice.**

Subhdeep belongs to a Scheduled Caste family (also known as 'Dalits') which makes her not only poor, but socially disadvantaged. Technically, 'caste' does not exist at all in the Sikh religion, which she belongs to. But on ground, the practice continues. From an early age, a Dalit child starts believing that she is a little 'less equal'. And born, to serve.

What's more, Subhdeep's father was a driver but he didn't have regular work. And he was addicted to alcohol. Being the eldest child, the burden of feeding the family had to be shared by Subhdeep. Although she accepted her lot, it certainly took a toll on her, both physically and mentally. She did not feel like talking to other children, or playing with them.

*"School mein bhi padhaai mein sabse peeche reh jaati thi."* (I fell behind in my studies as well.)

Eventually, Subhdeep simply stopped going to school. What was the point? Girls like her had little hope of a future... But things were about to change...

*"Tu chalegi Children Group mein?"* one of the girls in the village asked Subhdeep. "*Mazaa aayega... aaja!*" (Come to the Children's Group... it is fun.)

Subhdeep had no idea what this was, but went out of curiosity. The Children's Group in Jhandawala village of Bathinda district, Punjab had been set up the previous year. The kids met once a month and shared any problem they had been facing. And then tried to find a solution. As this was Subhdeep's first meeting, she just sat quietly.

Until a kind didi asked, "*Apne baare mein kuch batao...* what do you do? Where do you study?"

Subhdeep turned beetroot red. How was she to say, in front of so many people, that she didn't even attend school anymore? But during this meeting, she heard - for the first time - that *bachchon ke bhi adhikaar hote hain* (children also have rights). Which meant that she - Subhdeep - also had rights.

"I felt so happy… because I never knew that *bachchon se kaam karwana jurm hai."* (Child labour is wrong and illegal.)

The Children's Group decided to visit Subhdeep's home and talk to her parents. Initially, they were skeptical and even a little hostile.

"Subhdeep is my daughter… you cannot tell me what she can do, or can't do!" said her mother.

It took several months of counselling and cajoling to convince her that child labour is morally wrong. And it is also an offence under the law. Finally, in August 2015, 14 year old Subhdeep was re-enrolled* in the government school in her village, in class 7. Her parents made a commitment to not send her for *narma chugai* that winter.

"*Wo din mere liye sabse badi khushi ka din tha*!" (That was the happiest day of my life.)

---

* between 2014–18, the Ikea-Save the Children project in Punjab and Haryana removed a total of 1.1 lakh children from various forms of labour and put them into school.

Gradually, there was a change in Subhdeep's demeanour and her self-image. She became more confident and outgoing. Started participating in extra-curricular activities like music and dance.

And became an active member of the Children's Group which meets once a month in the panchayat bhavan and takes up a range of issues.

Such as getting Aadhaar cards made, or raising awareness about the ill-effects of beating children.

The campaign '*Komal haath, kalam ke saath*' (Little hands should hold pens) is especially close to Subhdeep's heart. As it directly addresses the problem of child labour during the cotton-picking season.

"We take a pledge from the parents *ki na karenge, na karne denge."* (We won't send our child to work, nor let others do so.)

Subhdeep's parents admit that it was tough, initially. As they missed the money Subhdeep would contribute. But over time, they realised it was for the best. Her father quit drinking and became more responsible while her mother also started participating in the local *mahila mandal*

DETROIT

"All children should study, no child should be involved in labour. It is the right of every child to study."

(women's group). And she is proud of her daughter's achievements.

A student of class 10, Subhdeep is well recognised by her principal, teachers and classmates. She talks about child rights in her school assembly and was felicitated as a 'role model' during the Independence Day celebrations. Subhdeep is also working at the district and state level. In fact, she has received training in theatre and how to make video films, in order to be more effective.

And, she has ambitious dreams for herself and what her future can be.

"*Mera challenge hai ki main naukri zaroor karoongi!*" (I know that I must take up a job.)

Subhdeep always wanted to become a teacher but now she's not so sure. She recently saw a film on television called 'Mumbai ki Kiran Bedi' and was highly inspired by it.

"I would like to end all the crimes in society!" she says, with idealistic fervour.

*My body is free, my mind is free…*
*I can see stars in the sky!*
*The time has come for me…*
*To think big and aim high.*

**ROSHANI BAIRWA**

Age 26, Mahmoodnagar Dhani (Rajasthan)

# FREE TO BE ME

She stood her ground against the tradition of child marriage. Roshani now campaigns against this practice which is still common in Rajasthan.

If only my father were still alive, Roshani often thought, my life would be so different.

"My childhood was filled with a lot of struggle… especially when it came to education."

Roshani's father passed away when she was just 2 years old; her mother got remarried. So the little girl was brought up by her dada-dadi (paternal grandparents). Though they did their best, dada was old and infirm. He eked out a living by grazing a few goats. And with that small income, the family somehow managed to stay afloat.

"Later, my grandfather adopted a distant relative and his family, to help in his old age."

Chacha-chachi (uncle-aunt) and their 3 sons were not very fond of Roshani. And they were of the opinion *ki ladki ki shaadi jald se jald ho jaaye* (it's best for a girl to be married off early). Back in 2006–7, this was a commonly held view in Mahmoodnagar Dhani, a small village in Peeplu tehsil of Tonk district in Rajasthan.

One fine day dada called Roshani and said her, "We have found a good match for you…"

Roshani was shocked. She was just 14 and not at all interested in getting married.

"But dada, I wish to study… at least till $12^{th}$ standard. Please… don't do this."

Dada shook his head. What did a little girl know about the harsh realities of life? As she blossomed into a young woman, it would be more and more difficult to keep her safe from lecherous elements. And *padhna likhna wo sab theek hai*, but an educated girl would need an educated groom… *wo kahan se milega?* (Where would such a fellow be found?)

The Bairwa community which Roshani belongs to is classified as a Scheduled Caste and mostly tills the land. They have large families and limited means of income. So from an economic point of view, dada was quite right….. But Roshani Bairwa was not one to just bow her head and accept her fate.

As a member of the Kalibai Bal Samooh (Children's Group) in her village, Roshani knew that 'child marriage' is wrong. So in the next meeting, she spoke up for herself.

"I am a member of this group, *mere saath galat ho raha hai* (it's wrong, what is happening to me). You must help me!"

The entire Bal Samooh (Children's Group) went to meet Roshani's grandfather but he was unmoved. So, members of the local NGO* which had formed the Children's Group also joined in. Finally, they managed to convince dada to postpone the wedding. Just before the lagan patrika (invitation card) was about to be printed.

Word spread like wildfire in the tiny hamlet of Mahmoodnagar Dhani.

"*Roshani ne apni shaadi rukwa di, Roshani ne apni shaadi rukwa di!*" (Roshani has stopped her own wedding.)

The samaaj was not pleased. Who was this young girl to challenge centuries-old tradition*? Something must be wrong with her… and why did her family allow this madness?

"Stay away from this witch," they told their daughters. In fact, Roshani's own uncle and aunt stopped talking to

---

* Shiv Shakti Samiti, Ranauli
* 40% of child marriages in the world are in India

her. But she took all this in her stride. In fact, she thought of herself as being 'lucky'. There were so many other girls who had not objected to their marriages and had even borne children at a young age.

**Who was this young girl to challenge centuries-old tradition?**

"If they cannot speak up, I must speak for them," decided young Roshani. And so she vigourosly took up this cause, along with members of the Bal Samooh. The group made door-to-door visits in their own village, and in the surrounding area, to talk about the ill-effects of early marriage.

In fact, at the time, 68% of girls in Rajasthan were getting married before the age of 18. This was despite the existence of a law which states that aiding and abetting child marriage is punishable with a fine of Rs 1 lakh and 2 years in prison. But implementation on the ground was very poor.

As awareness grew, some families decided to wait till their daughters turned 18. The rest just became smarter at hiding it.

But they didn't realise that the Bal Samooh had a secret weapon - the eyes and ears of children. One day a young boy came to the group meeting and gave an invitation card for the wedding of his sister Sonu. She was over the age of 18 - so there was no problem. They could all enjoy the festivities.

"*Lekin ek din pehle… meri chhoti behen Ranu ki bhi shaadi kar rahe hain*," he blurted. (One day prior, my younger sister Ranu will also be married.)

But Ranu was just 15! With this advance information, the kids landed up at the pandal. The family denied there was any such plan but Roshani and her friends refused to budge from there. Just to ensure no hush-hush pheras* could take place. And finally, they succeeded.

Over time, Roshani was able to prevent 15 child marriages and became a role model in Tonk district. She received the 'Laadli Samman' award from the state government and was even roped in to be a brand ambassador for women and child rights during the 2015 national election campaign.

---

* walk around the sacred fire which solemnises Hindu weddings

"When people realised that girls are standing up against child marriage it helped to bring an end to the practice."

WELCOME

The SDM* of Tonk was so impressed with Roshani that he declared in a public meeting, "You are a beti (daughter) of the entire state, we will support your further education."

Roshani went on to complete her BA from a degree college in Tonk, and Master's in Social Work from Banasthali Vidyapeeth. Financial support came from her local NGO, a corporate foundation as well as members of her own community. The Bairwas - who once ostracised the girl who took a stand against traditions - now look up to her and ask for advice.

"*Meri bachchi 17 saal 10 mahine ki hai… abhi shaadi kar dein kya?*" (My daughter is 17 years and 10 months old, is it okay to get her married?)

When Roshani counselled them to wait another 2 months, they readily agreed. After all, no one wants the headache of police and NGOs visiting their homes…This is not to say child marriage has been completely abolished. A poor family may still prefer to get all their girls married on the same day, with a single wedding feast. But certainly, it's less common now.

---

* SDM - sub-divisional magistrate (high ranking government officer)

Roshani now works with the Sakhi Centre in Tonk, set up by the state government to tackle issues of women, including dowry and domestic violence. She continues to educate and raise awareness, using kathputli karyaram (puppet show), a medium unique to Rajasthan. In one such performance the girl sings to her father:

*Bapu chhoti si umar mein parnayejo mati na*

*Meri jindagi no dhool mein milayeje mati na*

(Father, don't marry me at a young age

Don't ruin my life in that way....)

At the end of such a show, a 'dev ki jyot' (sacred lamp) is passed around, with parents taking a pledge to not marry their daughters before the age of 18. And more and more girls are now completing their schooling, thanks to state government schemes which award a bicycle to girls who pass class 8$^{th}$, laptop for class 10 and Scooty after class 12.

"So much change is visible… in just 10 years," says Roshani. "*Lekin aagey aur bhi bahut kuch karna hai.*" (There is still a lot of work to do…)

*A world where children are free,*
*where they have a voice.*
*Where there is harmony and respect,*
*and plenty of choice.*

**RUMI KUMARI**

Age 24, Burmu, (Jharkhand)

# INTO THE LIGHT

She was born in poverty but rose above her circumstances through education. Rumi now guides other girls who wish to do the same.

Rumi was born in Burmu, a village in Jharkhand, to a family which had too many mouths to feed.

"My parents were illiterate, they worked in the fields all day without any fixed payment. So we never knew where our next meal is coming from…"

On a good day, Rumi's mother came home with half a kg of rice and some saag (greens). But on other days, there was only starch water, left over from cooking the rice. Rumi and her 7 siblings often went to bed hungry.

Given these circumstances, the family was keen that all their children start working.

Every morning, as Rumi headed out to gather firewood, she passed by the boys and girls heading to school. Her heart longed to be join them but her parents could not see any point in enrolling her. Then, they heard about something called the 'mid-day meal' *.

"My mother thought, she will get something to eat… so for that, I was sent to school."

---

* As per a judgement passed by the Supreme Court in 2001, every government school in India must provide a free meal to its students at lunchtime.

But it didn't last long. When she was about 9 years old, Rumi got an attractive offer. A man known to the family said there was a job with a family based in Simdega.

"You work a little in the morning, and you can go to school in the afternoon," he promised.

***Pehle mere andar himmat nahin thi* (I had no courage.)**

Well, it sounded good to innocent young Rumi. She went to Simdega willingly, looking forward to a 'better life'. But the reality was quite different. All they wanted thc little girl to do was was sweep the floors, wash the dishes, clean the toilets. And remain quiet, invisible.

One day Rumi asked, "What about the promise of sending me to school?"

"Admission is closed right now, we will do it next time," they said.

When the new session was starting, Rumi once again asked, "Can I join school now?"

This time, she received a tight slap on her face. That day, Rumi resolved to somehow leave and go back home. She told her employer she was homesick.

"Send me home please, I will come back in a day or two,"

Surprisingly, they agreed, and put her on the bus. She was dropped off some distance from the village, with no money and no clue how to where to go. An elderly man on a motorbike saw her crying and stopped to ask what was the matter.

He said, "Don't worry, I will make sure you reach home safely."

It was past 8 pm when Rumi reached Burmu village. Though happy to see her, the parents thought it would be best if she returned to work. A month later, Rumi was sent to another household, this time in Patna.

"I ran away from there also, and this time I said I will never go back."

When Rumi told her parents she wanted to return to her studies, they were skeptical. Instead, they decided to get her married to a 15 year old boy, from a neighbouring village.

10-year-old Rumi stood her ground.

"Marriage will not lead me anywhere... see what it's done to my sisters!" she said.

All 4 of them were 'settled' but what did that really mean? The eldest was married at age 6 and gave birth to a child at age 11. The child was weak and sickly. It was the same story repeated over and over again.

Rumi knew just one thing - this would not be *her* story.

She had heard of a residential school for girls like herself, from poor families, and decided to find out more. Admission to this school was in the hands of 'BO sir' - the Block Education Officer.

She went one morning and spent the whole day, waiting outside his office. Then a second day and a third day. But Rumi was not one to give up. Finally, on the fourth day, she got a brief audience.

"Sir, please help me! I am very keen to study and this school is my only hope!"

The officer gave her a patient hearing and said he would help. A month later, there was no news. Rumi's mother taunted her.

"I told you - these are just castles in the air. Nothing will come of it."

"I know I will get admission… just wait and see," Rumi replied, with quiet confidence.

And sure enough, it happened. Having completed class 4, Rumi was expecting to join class 5. But the only seat available in Kasturba Gandhi Vidyalaya, Burmu was in class 8. Which meant she would have to work twice as hard as any other student. Was the little girl prepared for this? Would she be able to cope?

"I will do whatever it takes," she said, in all sincerity. And was given a chance.

The first few days at the boarding school went in a daze. Rumi was shy and scared to speak to anyone. One of the cooks in the mess happened to be from her village.

"When you feel lonely, come to the kitchen," said the kindly man.

"I am now recognised by everyone in the village because of the awards I have won... Even the Sarpanch listens to what I have to say."

Save the Children
THE CHANGEMAKER AWARD
Rumi Kumari
IN IRANI

So Rumi would go and help with the cutting of vegetables. And slowly, she grew confident enough to approach some of her teachers. With their help, she secured a 'C' grade in class 8. While another child may have felt disheartened, Rumi was motivated to do better. *Haar maanane ka sawaal hi nahin…*

"I was determined to get a 1st division in class 9… with hard work, I managed 2nd division!"

On Saturdays and Sundays the girls would crowd around the TV to watch serials and Bollywood films. Only Rumi stayed in her room, or in the library.

"Why don't you join your friends?" her teacher asked.

"Ma'am. I am the weakest in my class so I don't want to waste my time watching TV. Please give 4-5 questions and I will try to answer them!"

*Mehnat ka phal meetha hota hai.* In class 10, Rumi stood 9th among 35 children - a hard-won and well-deserved achievement.

That same year, there was another development. Vikas Bharti foundation visited the school and conducted a training program.* Rumi enjoyed the classes, conducted by didis, who talked to the girls in a friendly manner. Boosted their confidence. And made them realise that by working together problems could be solved.

"I was selected as a charcha leader (discussion leader) in the Bal Sansad (Child Parliament)."

This group met every Saturday and identified what issues were bothering various children. It could be something simple, like lack of sanitary napkins. Or something much bigger…

"I shared my story with the group. And after the training, many girls got the courage to stop child marriage in their home, or in their village."

Even as Rumi flourished in her new role, a burning question remained. What would happen after class 12? Her family did not have the means to fund any further education…It was her mentor at Vikas Bharti who then told her about 'Saksham'. These are skill development courses run by the government, free of cost, with assured job placement.

---

* Lalita and Babu training module developed by Save the Children

"We will provide you with hostel accommodation in Ranchi," he said. "*Koi chinta ki baat nahin.*"

Despite this assurance, Rumi's mother was against her going to Ranchi. *Bade sheher mein kuch bhi ho sakta hai* (the big city is dangerous for girls). But Rumi was adamant. She had come 4th in her class in the 12th standard board exam. Many girls had dropped out along the way, and few would have this chance to do a vocational course and start working.

"*Aisa mauka baar baar nahin aata* (very few get such an opportunity)... how could I could let it go?"

In June 2017, Rumi joined the Vikas Bharti hostel in Ranchi. She completed a beautician course, with 30 other girls, under the expert guidance of Namrata ma'am.

"Ma'am taught us well and even encouraged us that you can open your own parlour!"

But by the end of the course Rumi realised - she did not want to be a beautician. Her dream was to study further, get a college degree. With the help of Vikas Bharti, Rumi secured admission in Ram Lakhan college for a B.A. While she has subjects like Geography, History and Nagpuri*, her major is Political Science.

"I was asked to stand for elections in my college... but I refused. As I wanted to focus on my studies."

Unlike most students in her class, Rumi wakes up at 4 am and 'goes to work' at 5.30 am (at the reception of Vikas Bharti). This job gives her pocket money, so she can fully support herself. Since the workload is light, she often uses the time to study. At 10 am, Rumi is off to college. And in the evenings - unless there are exams - she's back on duty at the Vikas Bharti office.

In addition, Rumi is in constant touch with the girls in her village. She is a role model who is often asked for advice on admission to school or skill training programs.

"My sister, my niece, my cousin and many other village girls I have helped, to join Kasturba hostel."

Six girls from her village came to Ranchi for training under the Saksham Jharkhand Kaushal Vikas Yojana. Some have stayed back to work and are supporting their families, financially.

---

* Nagpuri is one of 22 dialects spoken in Jharkhand

Their parents now say, "*Aap humko naya soch, naya jeevan diye hain.*" (You have given us a new way of thinking, new life.)

Rumi's mother no longer worries when Rumi will get married. Nor does she oppose her travelling to faraway Delhi or Bangalore, to represent the cause of children.

Reflecting on her journey, Rumi says, "*Pehle mere andar himmat nahin thi.*" (I had no courage.)

Now she does not hesitate to call the media to highlight an injustice. Or speak her mind in front of the Chief Minister. For it is small acts of resistance that create big changes in society.

And Rumi plans to keep insisting and keep resisting, until her last breath.

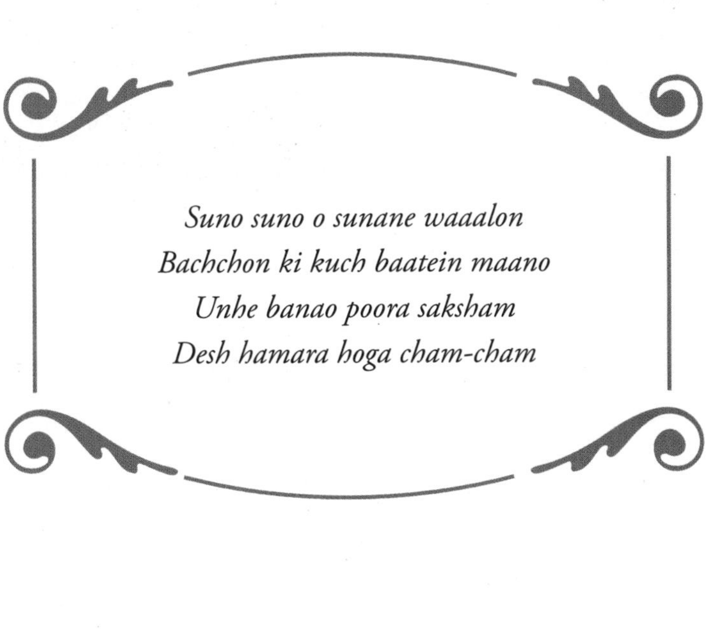

*Suno suno o sunane waaalon*
*Bachchon ki kuch baatein maano*
*Unhe banao poora saksham*
*Desh hamara hoga cham-cham*

SARASWATI KUMARI DHANUK

Age 16, EJC Basti (Kolkata)

# POWERPUFF GIRL

Filth and fear were a way of life in her slum. Saraswati and her Shaktimaan group worked hard to change that.

Saraswati lives in EJC Basti, an illegal slum that has developed in the port area.

"My hut lies beneath a bridge and is almost always surrounded by large container trucks."

Children play hide and seek under these lorries -- which is dangerous - but there is no other space. 1300 families reside in this slum, near the under-construction Metro line in Taratalla, on land belonging to Kolkata Port Trust and the Railways. Most of the residents are migrants from Bihar, UP and Jharkhand.

No slum is a pleasure to live in, but EJC Basti is a little worse than other slums. As it is illegal, it can be razed to the ground at any time. Hence, most residents live in shanties and never make a pucca home. There are little or no municipal services. Stray animals roam around freely and so do unscrupulous elements.

"*Yahan ka mahaul acchha nahin hai* (the atmosphere in our area is not good)... especially for girls."

Saraswati studies in class 12. To reach her school she has to catch a local train for a few minutes ride and then walk for about 15 minutes from the station to the school.

When it rains, and it rains quite often in Kolkata, her life is a mess. Her house is a mess, with water seeping in from all sides.

But what is most problematic for Saraswati is her white-coloured school uniform getting stained with mud, with her shoes and socks completely wet. She gets scolded for turning up like that.

"But what can I do – not going to school is also not a good option!"

Saraswati knows how much of a blessing it is for girls like her to get an education. She had dropped out of school at some point and no one really cared. *Nahin padhna hai to mat padh!* (It's no big deal if you don't want to study). Then, one afternoon, she saw a bright yellow bus parked a stone's throw from her house.

**We formed a children's group called Shaktimaan* which meets every Sunday**

It was a Mobile Learning Centre (MLC), created with a simple objective - to identify children who had dropped out of school. And rekindle in them a love for learning.

---

* a popular comic book hero

Along with books, pencils, toys and teachers, the mobile van brought with it new ideas, such as 'child rights'. This was all very new and interesting for Saraswati.

"We formed a Children's Group called Shaktimaan which meets every Sunday."

Once a month, the kids invite leaders from their area, as well as mothers and guardians, for the Sunday meeting. They share the work that Shaktimaan group* is doing, and what kind of support they need from the elders. In addition, the kids talk about the importance of polio vaccination, iron tablets and nutritious food for mother and child.

Shaktimaan group conducted a survey of the basti (slum) and found there were 13 children who did not attend school. Not only girls but several boys had dropped out of formal education. In fact, they were employed by local garages, to paint cars. This, Saraswati knew, was wrong. Every child under the age of 14 must be in school!

"We spoke to their parents and 10 children were able to start going to school again!"

---

* a collaborative effort of Sarva Shiksha Mission, the state government and Save the Children

EJC Basti is plagued by many issues, one of them was the kachcha (dirt) road which ran through the colony. It was basically mud and became a sea of slush during the rains. Now this was a problem that not only affected children, but all residents of the area. But it was Shaktimaan group which decided to 'do something' about it.

When the kids met, one of them came up with the idea of meeting Bobby Hakim, then Minister of Urban Development and Municipal Affairs.

"We will give him a letter, telling about all the problems in our basti… and he can get them fixed!"

The letter was carefully written in English and typed up with help from 'tuition sir'. They knew the area where the minister lived but not the exact address.

"We had to ask the traffic policeman for help… not once but 2–3 times."

When they finally reached Hakim's residence they saw that he was getting into his car.

"Uncle, *ruk jaaiye*! (Please stop for a minute)," Saraswati called out.

"*Kya hua beta*? (What is the matter)," asked the minister. He spent a few minutes with the children, asked them to give the letter to his Personal Assistant and promised to look into the matter.

Not that anything changed overnight but 3 years later, when you visit the slum, there is indeed a concrete road. And cleaner toilets. Some of which is due to the Swachh Bharat Abhiyan.*

But every little stone thrown into the water creates a ripple effect. The effect of Shaktimaan is being felt not only in the community but in the core of the family unit itself. Saraswati recalls how, earlier, her father was disappointed that he had two daughters and no sons. But as she started working with Shaktimaan, became bold and confident, his attitude changed.

"I told him that there have been many great women like Mother Teresa and Indira Gandhi.. so it's not that only boys can be smart!"

Saraswati's father now supports her completely. When he is invited to any function and people ask him how many boys he has, he points to his daughters and says, "These are my boys."

* Clean India Mission, a national campaign launched in 2014

"Our slum had kachcha (dirt) roads which caused a lot of hardship to everyone... so we children decided to write a letter and give it to our Minister, asking him to fix the problem."

Saraswati glows from the inside. And her desire to make a difference grows. She envisions a day when Shaktimaan can train women in her basti to make jute bags and sell them, to ease their financial woes. Saraswati is also inspired by Anoyara Khatun*, who leads more than 2000 children affiliated to 80 groups in the Sandeshkhali region of West Bengal.

"I want to be a leader and work to improve our country... which is still very backward."

Wise words for a young girl who goes by the name Saraswati**. May she succeed in her lofty aim.

* chapter 1 in this book
** In Hindu mythology, Saraswati is goddess of knowledge and wisdom

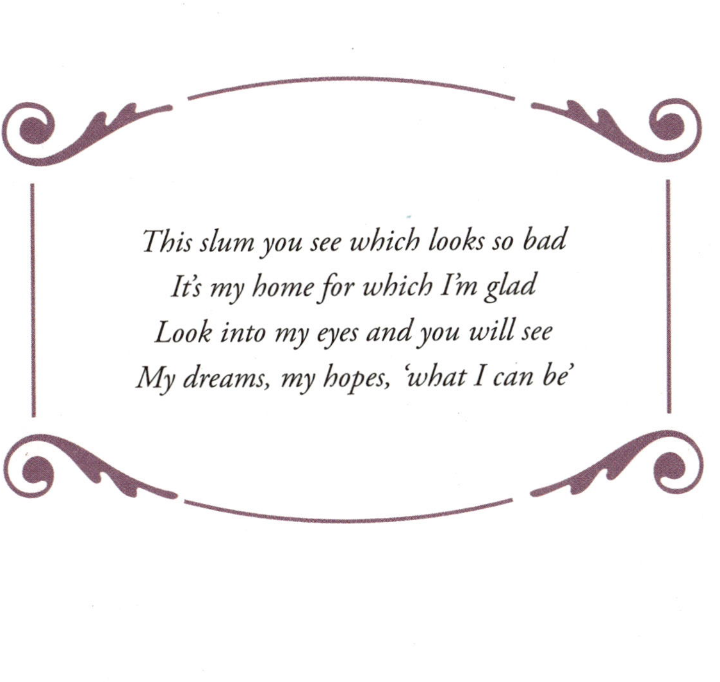

*This slum you see which looks so bad*
*It's my home for which I'm glad*
*Look into my eyes and you will see*
*My dreams, my hopes, 'what I can be'*

BADHENGE
We Will Grow

**SONI**

Age 18, Grant Road (Mumbai)

# IN HER OWN LEAGUE

A child of the streets, she had a bleak future. But that changed when Soni's talent for cricket got recognised.

Soni grew up in the midst of heat and dust, greed and lust, on the streets of Mumbai.

"My father is handicapped... he is in the village. My mother and grandmother look after me and my two sisters. They work really hard, so we can have a roof over our head..."

For many years, that roof was just a sheet of tarpaulin, on the side of the road, 200 metres from Grant Road station. In that tiny hovel, the two women and three children ate, slept, cooked and bathed, always living in fear of the next monsoon, or the next eviction.

"Nothing is free in Mumbai... we had to pay rent, even to live on the footpath."

When the heat became unbearable, Soni and her sisters would sleep outside, on a straw mat. One night a man started groping one of the girls. Luckily, the mother woke up and raised an alarm. The man fled, in haste. But who knows when the next pervert might come along.

"My grandmother used to stay awake all night... just to keep a watch over us."

Soni's grandmother is a tiny lady, less than 4 feet tall. She is bent over with age, her hands rough and calloused from washing dishes and swabbing floors. Some of these jobs were all the more difficult because she was afraid of using elevators. So she would climb up… all of 30 floors.

"*Meri nani jaisa koi nahin ho sakta* (there can be no one like my grandmother!)," exclaims Soni.

It was with blood, sweat and toil that Soni and her siblings were admitted to a private, English medium school in South Mumbai. Despite taking a good amount in fees, the school was under-equipped and under-staffed. They crammed in 70-80 pupils in a single class.

"I was not at all interested in studies… I thought it is of no use."

The only thing Soni was interested in, was gully cricket. Every evening she would join the rag-tag band of boys batting, bowling and fielding in the bylanes of Grant Road. She was the only girl but they didn't care - and neither did she. After all, she was a good player and that's all that mattered!

One day an older gentleman whom everyone knew as 'sir' came up to Soni.

He said, "I am a cricket coach. You know Ajinkya Rahane? He is my student…"

Soni was impressed. "*Ajinkya Rahane kya mast khelta hai*", she was thinking to herself. When, all of a sudden, 'sir' threw a googly.

"Soni, I would like to start coaching you. *Bolo, coaching join karogi*?"

That evening Soni went back to her shanty with a skip in her step and a song in her heart. *Sir mujhe coaching mein le rahe hain… mujhe*??? Never in her wildest dreams had she thought something like this would be possible.

Sir had explained to her - it's going to be hard work. You have to come to Oval maidan near Churchgate every morning, at 6.30. You will do warm up and then 'drill' for 3 hours. No matter what the weather conditions. Whether you have headache or stomach ache. No excuses.

"I will be there," Soni promised. And she was as good as her word.

People in the neighbourhood started whispering… "Why does she always play with boys?"…. "*Ladki bigad jayegi…* she will go astray!" But luckily, Soni's mother and grandmother were always supportive.

"If cricket is the one thing that brings my child happiness.. why not? Let her play!"

Playing became Soni's passion, her obsession, her addiction. Other girls her age were interested in fashion, jewellery and make-up. But Soni dreamt only of season balls and cricket bats, kneepads and helmets. And snow-white cricket clothing.

"I could not afford to buy any of it… but Sir arranged everything for me."

As her game went from strength to strength, Sir nudged her to try out for the under-16 state team. There were 400 girls who came for the selection. Soni gave it her best shot and made it, to the final list. It was perhaps the happiest moment of her life.

But everything came crashing down, with a thud.

As per the rules, Soni had to submit a document which had 'proof of residence'. The authorities asked for a ration card which Soni did not possess. The few documents her mother did have were destroyed when their shanty was flooded during monsoons.

"I have Aadhaar but… they said it's not enough."

It was a big blow for Soni but what to do - life must go on. And when one door closes, another somehow opens. Soni's younger sister Simran had a friend who told them about Salaam Baalak Trust. They run a day care centre for children, right next to Charni Road station.

"We visited the centre *aur hamein accha laga*."

The three sisters started coming to Salaam Baalak regularly. By this time Soni was in class 10 and due to appear for her Board Exams. Since she had never paid much attention to studies, she was expected to fail. And it was no big deal, really. *Padhaai karke kya hoga mera?*

The didis at Salaam Baalak Trust would not accept defeat so easily.

"I want to do well
in 12th standard,
so I can join Khalsa
college.. they have
a girls' cricket team!"

"You are smart, Soni. If you put some effort, you can pass. You can go to college!"

**I was not at all interested in studies... I thought it is of no use.**

They tutored her in Maths, which was her weak spot. They gave her practice with Hindi, which was also tough. And when she reached home there was Lakshmi didi, who lived nearby, ever ready to sit with Soni. And give her the helping hand she needed.

It was a rainy morning in June when the SSC results were declared.

"*Main pass ho gayi... pass ho gayi!!*" said Soni, when she entered the Salaam Baalak centre. Her eyes gleamed with pride and quiet confidence. It was a modest 48% but enough to get her admission into the commerce stream in a local junior college.

And now, she has her sights set on higher goals.

"I want to do well in 12th standard, so I can join Khalsa college... they have a girl's cricket team!"

Things are looking up for Soni, and her family. They now reside in a chawl, in an open area which has no doors or shutters. But it's so much better than living on the street. They are grateful.

"This time… when I try out for under-19 girls' team… I will have proof of residence," she says.

In the past, Soni used to work in people's homes, along with her mother, to supplement the family income. But now, with the help of Shahnaz didi from Salaam Baalak trust, she has got an internship in an investment company. Once she turns 18, they will give her a part-time job.

"This way she will be able to work and also complete her studies," says Shahnaz.

And, of course, play cricket. In the humid heat of April, Soni is up and awake at 5.30 am, so that she can reach Shivaji Park at 6.30 am. And do the 'drill'. She is training with other girls now, with a coach who charges a high fee. But not from Soni.

"I don't think all the girls are very serious… " she laughs. "*Par mere liye cricket hi sab kuch hai.*"

Soni recalls the days when she had long hair, which many people admired. But one morning she realised her hair was becoming a hindrance. It just wouldn't fit into her helmet. So she went to the barber and asked him to chop it off.

"This was the only time my grandmother got really upset… she didn't talk to me for 2 days!"

Soni knows she will be the talk of the town, the day she gets selected for the Indian team. Nothing less will do. Selection is a matter of performance, and a matter of luck. But you also need a strategy.

"These days I am focussing on bowling… because a good team always needs a good fast bowler!"

*Not long ago, Soni went to bed hungry.*
*Now, she is hungry to succeed.*
*A nudge, a push, a pat on the back.*
*Goes a long, long way indeed…*

**SALMAN**

Age 19, New Delhi

## ACT 2

He struggled with his emotions until he found an outlet in the medium of theatre. Salman now dreams of making it in Bollywood.

Salman was an angry young man, an anger that spilled out and burnt him in many different ways.

"My father left my mother, so she had to beg on the streets to survive."

Wanting a better life for her son, she sent Salman to live in a shelter from the age of one and a half. The Aman Biradari hostel for destitute children could provide a bed and meal to fill the little boy's stomach. But not the sense of being loved, that he craved for.

"I didn't like it when people spoke harshly to me, especially any teacher."

Salman constantly got into fights with authority figures. Once, it got so bad that he caught hold of a teacher's neck... Every such incident would only lead to more punishment and the only escape for Salman would be to run away. The question was where?

"Once, when I was 6 or 7 years old, I started working in a tea shop."

The job started at 5 in the morning and ended after midnight. As a chhotu*, he was paid just Rs 25 per day. At times, hot tea would fall in Salman's hands and scald them. The thing he feared most, though, was breaking a glass.

"The owner would deduct the cost of that glass from my wages."

This continued for 7 months, until he met some people who promised a 'better deal'. One where Salman could earn - not in hundreds - but thousands. But when he learnt that they wanted him to become a pickpocket, he refused point blank.

"I was very scared but somehow I managed to escape from their clutches."

Finding little solace in the outside world, Salman would eventually return to the shelter. And also, because his mother would implore him, to go back for her sake. She had little to offer Salman and his younger sister Shabnam (also growing up in a shelter).

"My mother somehow managed to sleep at night, in the Hanuman mandir complex."

---

* young helper

By this time, she was also earning a small income selling water packets at traffic signals. The cost price of each packet was 25 paise but it was no easy business. Braving the heat, the fumes and unkind jibes. Some went as far as snatching packets and zooming off, without paying.

"I remember once, there was an argument, and someone injured me with a knife..."

What hurt Salman the most was people being disrespectful to his mother. He recalls an incident where she was begging for alms and a shopkeeper flaunted a hundred rupee note in front of her. Then, he hurled some abuses, struck her in the face and asked them to 'get lost'.

"I felt my fingers curl up in my wrist, my blood was boiling..."

Salman could see tears well up in his mother's eyes. She did not react and simply led him away. But the young man could not bear this humiliation. He returned some hours later with a few of his friends, carrying firecrackers left over from Diwali. Which he lit and flung into the shop.

He waited until the shopkeeper and his salesmen came rushing out, startled and scared.

"You insulted my mother this morning... *uska jawab dene aaya hoon*!" he yelled at the man.

**These are my streets... it's where I feel most at home.**

In the darkest of times, all a man needs is a ray of hope. For Salman, that hope came in the form of music. A friend at the hostel challenged him to sing. For one whole month, Salman listened to songs on the radio and did *riyaaz* (practice) by himself.

"*Maine gaane mein usse takkar li*... and I was able to hold my own."

Every year, there is a festival of music at the Qutub Minar, where top singers perform for an elite audience. Salman dreamt of singing at this festival. Later, when the hostel shifted to Mehrauli, a senior called Akash encouraged him to pursue music. Treating him like a 'younger brother'.

It was too good to be true. Akash became possessive, as well as abusive. One day while Salman was practising on the harmonium the older boy slapped him, in front of everyone. Once again, there was no option but to run away. But to his dismay, *mummy bhi usey galat samajhne lagi.*

"I felt like doing suicide but because I loved my mother, I did not."

Finally, Salman was taken in by a different shelter (DMRC Children Home) and that's when an actual ray of sunshine pierced the clouds of despair. Pankaj bhaiyya - a volunteer with Salaam Baalak Trust asked Salman if he would like to take a shot at acting in a street play.

"I did not believe he would actually give me a chance…"

When you've been ejected, dejected and rejected on so many fronts, it's hard to recognise a genuine well-wisher. Salman's instinct was to get angry, to push this opportunity away. But Pankaj bhaiyya was not one to give up easily. Slowly but surely, he won Salman's trust.

"All my life I was told… *tum kisi layak ho nahin*… you are good for nothing!"

It was time to change that belief. The 13th of January, 2011 is a date Salman will never forget. That was the day

"There is almost no coverage of the problems of children. Media is obsessed with politicians and film stars – why would they talk about children, especially deprived children?"

he made his stage debut. It was a half-minute role in a five minute play. But in those 30 seconds, there was a transformation, a realisation.

"*Maine apne aap ko paana chahta tha…aur wo mujhe haasil hua.*" (I discovered my true self.)

The anger, the hurt and the pain, it was all channeled into that performance.

The audience gave Salman a standing ovation. An actor was born.

Over the next few years, Salman became an integral part of the Salaam Baalak troupe, whose mission is to spread awareness of child rights through street plays. They perform in slums, or on roadsides, in the blazing mid-day sun. Which doesn't bother Salman at all.

"These are my streets… it's where I feel most at home."

The roles he enjoys the most are those which are similar, to his own life story. At the age of 14, Salman played his first lead role in a play titled *Jisne Khoja Usne Paya*. It's the story of a boy called Qadir who goes out to find his destiny.

Another successful play was *Main Bhi to Bachcha Hoon* about a boy who is not allowed to go to school because his father wants him to work, earn money. Salman knows he's been lucky to have a mother who fought like a tigress, to keep him in school.

"*Wo unki himmat thi*... she did not let me to do menial jobs, even if it meant going to sleep hungry."

Acting has given Salman confidence, it has given him amazing opportunities. He was one of 30 kids selected to receive intensive training from P K Sharma, a Bollywood veteran. And through this platform, he got a chance to play a small role in the film *Bhaag Milkha Bhaag*.*

More small roles followed, until Salman got his 'big break' in *Paharganj*, where he plays a gangster with a heart of gold. The film didn't do well at the box office but that didn't dampen Salman's spirits.

"*Is line mein aisa hi hota hai*... " (Nothing comes easy in this line of work.)

---

* as Milkha's childhood friend

While acting remains a passion, Salman is also appearing for his 10th class board exams. He knows that he must complete graduation, in order to join the National School of Drama (NSD). And that, someday, he *will* get there.

*The fire within is now tempered with hope.*
*The power and passion of a dream.*
*What lies ahead we do not know.*
*But faith in oneself must reign supreme.*

**SUMIT**

Age of 15, Bhanwar Singh Camp (New Delhi)

## MANN KI BAAT

He grew up in a tough place. But those difficulties have inspired Sumit to compose original, cause-based rap music.

As a child Sumit spent long, hot sweaty summers without fans, coolers or air conditioning.

"Actually the electricity would be gone the whole day," he recalls. "There was also severe shortage of water."

In Bhanwar Singh Camp, the slum colony where Sumit resides, women would queue up early in the morning to fill buckets at the few hand pumps. And fights broke out frequently, over who got how much. Meanwhile in the posh residential colony of Vasant Kunj, a stone's throw away, lawns were being watered with hosepipes. And homes buzzed with air-conditioners.

Yet, the kids of Bhanwar Singh Camp were not resentful, sullen or bitter. They had their own ways of having fun.

"We used to play cricket in the hot sun.... I used to dream of becoming like M S Dhoni," he grins.

Then one day an NGO called 'Magic Bus' came to the camp, and Sumit got to involved in a new sport - 'football'. That was pretty cool! But the coolest thing in Sumit's life was something else...One of his older cousins was into music. Hanging out with bhaiyya, Sumit discovered a whole new world. The world of rap.

"I came to know about rappers like Ikka and Badshah.... who rap in Hindi language! And I got extremely inspired."

Sumit always had an interest in music, but he didn't think he had a good singing voice make it to some show like 'Indian Idol'! But with rap, the melody didn't really matter. It was all about the content of the lyrics and your style of delivery. If you had something to say, people would listen. But what should one write about?

Most of the Indian rap songs are about beautiful girls and expensive cars. But Sumit didn't want to join that bandwagon.

"*Wo to koi bhi likh sakta ha*i (anyone can do that!)," he thought.

Besides, he had no experience of that kind of life! What he *did* know was the slum life, so that's what he decided to write about. And this is how the words came out.

*Paani* (Water)

*Maane ya na maane hamari ye kahaniyan*
*Bhanwar singh camp ki ye zindagaaniyan*
*Purani jaani mani suni hain kai ki zubaniyaan*

*(Whether you believe it or not*
*This is the story of life in Bhanwar Singh Camp*
*Everyone here knows this since a long time)*

*Suraj se pehle hamari subah hoti hai*
*Chaar baje se duniya jung shuru hoti hai*

*(We wake up before sunrise*
*The fight (for water) starts from then)*

*Shauch ki yahan samsya badi hai*
*Chhoti chhoti galiyon mein janta badi hai*
*Boond boond paani aur line hain bahi hai*

*(The lack of toilets is a big problem here*
*In these small lanes there is a large population*
*Every drop of water is precious and lines are long)*

At the local Children's Group where he was an active volunteer, Sumit recited his jugalbandi (rhyme). The group mentor was impressed.

"Will you perform at the Independence Day celebration on August 15th?"

Sumit readily agreed - he had no jitters or stage fright. The performance created quite a stir, and even got him a cash award.

"Everyone appreciated my song... in fact they started asking me, tell us what you are writing next!"

**My inspiration to rap comes from the harsh experiences of my life.**

Well, that was over 2 years ago and there's been no looking back. The young man has been invited to rap at numerous community events, at school functions and children's forums.

In his free time, Sumit is busy penning down his thoughts, in the form of lyrics. He scribbles out the lines in his notebook and shares whatever he writes with friends. But only after he's recited each new creation to his mother. A simple lady who's lovingly brought up 4 kids and takes great pride in their progress.

"Earlier I used to think *yeh kya badbad hai par ab main bhi iski fan ban gayi hoon*!" (I didn't understand this style of singing but now I too am his fan.)

Sumit often hangs out in the tiny kitchen which is directly above the family's single-room house.

He might chew on a carrot or dig into a tomato, as he wrestles with which words to include in his song. Words that are easy to understand but also have meaning, and power. And that can have real impact on the minds of people.

"When you just say do like this, do like that - nobody listens. But when you give the message in the form of a song, *asar padta hai.*" (It connects with the public.)

One of Sumit's recent songs was on the topic of cleanliness, which is currently a national campaign. The lyrics go as follows:

*Sab.. apne gharon ko to saaf rakhte hain*
*Par galiyon mein gandgi failate hain*
*Kai bimaariyon se ghir jaate hain*

*(Everyone keeps their home clean*
*But throws garbage on the streets*
*And this creates disease)*

"When you just say do this, do that - nobody listens. But when you give the message in the form of a song, it connects with the public."

BEAST MODE

*Dilli ko isse upar uthana hai*
*Dilli hai rajdhani hamein rajdhani Dilli ko banana hai*
*(Delhi must rise above this*
*Delhi is our capital city, we have to make it beautiful)*

There has been visible improvement in the garbage situation at Bhanwar Singh Camp. And this song has played its role in changing mindsets.

In fact, life as a whole has seen drastic change and improvement in the last 2–3 years. Due to efforts of the local administration, Bhanwar Singh Camp now enjoys uninterrupted power supply. Water scarcity is a thing of the past and there's even a community toilet, with bio-digester and solar panels on the rooftop. Of course, there's no dearth of topics to rap about.

*School ki life hoti hai mazedaar*
*Thodi karte badmasshi thodi karte ladaai*
*(School life is fun*
*We are naughty and sometimes, we fight)*

*Teacher ke yahan karte hain padhaai*
*Ek baat samajh nahin aati hai*
*Saari padhai kyun sar ke oopar se jaati hai*
*(Teachers make us study*

*But one thing I don't understand*
*Is why do all the subjects go right over my head!)*

When he performed this song at school, his classmates went wild. Because that's exactly how *they* felt. The ability to connect with people - through song and in real life - is Sumit's greatest asset.

The release of the film 'Gully Boy'* was a lucky break for the 14-year-old. He was invited on the TV channel 'Delhi Aaj Tak' and subsequently, on many radio stations. What's more, he got a chance to meet his idol - Ikka Singh! The rapper encouraged Sumit to 'keep writing good songs' which the public can enjoy.

Though it would be easy for Sumit to also start singing about *pyaar* and *yaar* (love and friendship), he plans to stick to issue-based songs for now.

"*Rapper insaan tab banta hai jab unke oopar bahut saari cheez beetati hai.*" (You become a rapper when you've had a lot of harsh experiences in life.)

Apart from his own life, Sumit also looks to current events for inspiration. He wrote a rap on women's safety

---

* 2019 Bollywood film about a rapper in Mumbai's Dharavi slum

inspired by Nirbhaya and more recently, on faujis (after the Pulwama attack on armymen).

This talent was noticed by someone at the Aam Aadmi Party, who then approached Sumit to write a campaign song for the general elections. They were willing to pay handsomely, for each line.

However, Sumit aka 'DJ Kaku' declined the offer.

"We discussed it at home and my uncle said no - 'you are too young to get into politics' - *toh phir main nahin gaya* (I did not go for it)!"

Sumit's dream is to make it big - as a rap musician. He plans to start a YouTube channel. A friend is teaching him how to mix in the right beats, to enhance his rap. And soon he will be able to use a studio in Trilokpuri to do the needful. Meanwhile, Sumit is constantly cooking up new lyrics in his head...

*Some see the world as dreary and full of despair*
*I say it's beautiful but needs some repair*

# ACKNOWLEDGEMENTS

It would have been impossible to meet these amazing, often 'invisible', children without the support of numerous staff at Save the Children and its partners. Our gratitude goes out to **Bidisha Pillai** (CEO) and **Vishal Chowla** (COO) for encouraging this book. It was the Campaigns team: **Pragya Vats**, **Rachit Sharma** and **Sreepoorna Majumdar** who were a constant support during this project. A special thanks to the staff members who introduced the children to us: **Anisha Ghosh, Asma Dhar, Avinash Singh, Bipin Kumar, Chittapriyo Sadhu, Hemant Acharya, Jatin Mondar, Mahadev Hansda, Moumita Saha, Nagayya, Neha Sabharwal, Nilesh Nikade, Rafay Hussain, Rupali Goswamy, Sanjay Singh, Sharif Bhat, Soumi Halder, Suhail and Vikas Gora**. Truly, you are all child champions!

Thanks to the young photographer **Raghav Chowla** for taking photographs of some of the children in this book.

The authors also acknowledge the valuable contribution of **Varsha A Shah** at Bushfire Publishers, **Abhijit Mahida** for proofreading, **Krupal** and team (Thomson Press) and m/s Prakash Books India Pvt Ltd.

Save the Children is a leading international child rights organisation that works in 120 countries since 1919. In India they work in 9 states and were registered as Bal Raksha Bharat in 2008. In the last decade they have made a positive change to the lives of more than 1 crore (10 million) Indian children.

Save the Children has a bold ambition: it believes in a world in which all children survive, have the chance to learn, and are protected from abuse, neglect and exploitation.

It is relentlessly advocating for better policies for children and working with Government programmes, engaging with children and their communities and working to change the social ecosystem to meet its goals for children.

Save the Children/Bal Raksha Bharat is working towards reaching 4 million of the most deprived children across India between 2019–2021.

They are the true champions for children.
www.savethechildren.in
Follow on Twitter (@stc_india), Facebook (india.savethechildren) & Instagram (@savethechildren_india)